The Voice of
ENLIGHTENED
NUNS
THE THERIGATHA

One of the books of the Pali Canon
Found in the Khuddaka Nikāya

A translation into English from the Sinhala translation
by Venerable Kiribathgoda Gnānānanda Thera

A Mahamegha Publication

The Voice of Enlightened Nuns: the Therīgāthā
by Venerable Kiribathgoda Gnānānanda Thera

Published February 2016

Computer Typesetting by

Mahamevnawa Buddhist Monastery, Toronto
Markham, Ontario, Canada L6C 1P2
Telephone: 905-927-7117

www.mahamevnawa.ca

Published by

Mahamegha Publishers
Waduwawa, Yatigaloluwa, Polgahawela, Sri Lanka.
Telephone: +94 37 2053300 | 77 3216685
www.mahameghapublishers.com
mahameghapublishers@gmail.com

Contents

Section of Three Verses

Section of Four Verses

Section of Five Verses

Section of Six Verses

Section of Seven Verses

Section of Eight Verses

Section of Nine Verses

Section of Eleven Verses

Section of Twelve Verses

Section of Sixteen Verses

Section of Twenty Verses

Section of Thirty Verses

Section of Forty Verses

The Great Section

Introduction

The Arahant

It is sweet even to hear the sound of the word "Arahant." To be able to meet a venerable Arahant monk or nun is an extremely fortunate event. In this human world, living among the humans, walking on this earth, these Arahants belong to a group of marvelous humans.

Arahants Cannot Be Measured

In this universe, these magnificent beings only appear with the help of a fully enlightened Buddha. This is because it is only under the instruction of the Buddha that the Noble Eight-Fold Path which leads to the attainment of the fruit of Stream-entry, Once-returning, Non-returning, and Arahantship is revealed. Therefore it is impossible to measure these Arahants who have achieved the ultimate purity, having destroyed all defilements.

> "Monk Upasīva, there is no way to measure an Arahant who has achieved ultimate freedom, Nibbāna. If someone uses an ordinary unit of measurement to measure ordinary people, Arahants cannot be measured in this way. Once all defilements have been eradicated, all arguments cease."

Upasīva Sutta, Sutta Nipāta verse 1076

Like Golden Swans

For an ordinary person, it is impossible to comprehend the life of Arahants. An Arahant's life is unimaginably peaceful, simple, and liberated. In this world the only person that walks with perfect freedom is an Arahant. In this time period the very first person to become an Arahant was the fully enlightened Buddha. The Buddha spoke about the lives of Arahants in this way:

> "Arahants are well established in the Four Establishments of Mindfulness. They are not bound by craving. Like the swans that fly away from the lake, they let go of everything, large and small."

> *Dhammapada, verse 91*

The Tamed Arahant

If the six sense bases are completely tamed in someone, that person is definitely an Arahant. The tameness that arises from virtue, concentration, and wisdom is mind-blowing. This is the exact reason that they are extremely humble.

> "Arahants tame their senses with the same skill that an expert horse tamer tames his horses. Because of this they become utterly extinguished. Humble and with unshakeable minds, these unblemished Arahants are a pleasant sight, even for the gods."

> *Dhammapada, verse 94*

Beautiful Is the Place They Reside

The Arahant sages who do wholesome actions, who speak wholesome words, and who think wholesome thoughts, make even the environment around them become beautiful. The liberated personality of these Arahant monks and nuns matches the beauty of nature very well. Like the beauty of a flower, they possess an untarnished, inherent beauty.

"Whether it be a village, a jungle, a valley, a hill or any other place, if Arahants dwell there, that place is truly delightful."

Dhammapada, verse 98

Glowing with Wisdom

Possessing an enchanting wisdom, our Great Teacher, the Buddha, shared his knowledge with his disciples. Those disciples used the power of the Buddha's enchanting wisdom to stimulate their own wisdom. It was because of that power of wisdom that they were able to rise above the ordinary people. The Buddha explained that point in this way:

"A beautiful, fragrant lotus blooms in a mud-hole filled with filth along the highway road. In the same way, in the world with its ignorant, worldly people that have stained and impure beliefs, a disciple of the Buddha will stand out among them, shining with brilliant wisdom."

Dhammapada, verses 58 & 59

The Realization of an Arahant

One becomes an Arahant by realizing the Four Noble Truths fully. That realization must occur in three phases and twelve modes. The Blessed One explained this fact in his very first discourse—the Dhammacakkappavattana Sutta.

When one becomes a stream enterer, that disciple attains the first phase with regard to the Four Noble Truths. It is known as "the knowledge of the truth."

The Knowledge of the Truth

The one who attained the Knowledge of the Truth embraces the first factor of the Noble Eight-fold Path. This means he has within himself the right view that comes from the understanding of the Four Noble Truths. He knows by his own understanding: suffering as a noble truth, the cause of suffering as a noble truth, the end of suffering as a noble truth, and that the path that must be followed to end suffering is the Noble Eight-fold Path as a noble truth. This is the Knowledge of the Truth.

The Knowledge of the Task to Be Accomplished

This is the second phase. In the first phase, the disciple understood the knowledge of the truth with regards to the Four Noble Truths. In this second phase, the disciple should have the knowledge of the task to be accomplished with regard to each noble truth. He understands that the noble truth of suffering is to be fully understood, the noble truth of the cause of suffering is to be abandoned, the noble truth of the end of suffering is to be realized, and the way leading to the end of suffering is to be developed in terms of virtue, concentration, and wisdom. This way the disciple of the Buddha realizes the Four Noble Truths completely, having established on the knowledge of the Four Noble Truths itself.

The Knowledge That the Task Has Been Completed

In this way, when one has started to develop the Noble Eightfold Path, he is capable of developing the thirty-seven aids to enlightenment. Within it, the three-fold way of training called virtue, concentration, and wisdom is developed. Then, he becomes liberated from all defilements and becomes enlightened. Having completed the task with regard to the Four Noble Truths he possesses the Knowledge That the Task Has Been Completed.

This means he has the knowledge that what had to be done with regard to the Noble Truth of Suffering has been completed. That is, the complete understanding of the Noble Truth of Suffering. He has the knowledge that what had to be done with regard to the Noble Truth of the Cause of Suffering has been completed. That is, the complete eradication of the Noble truth of the Cause of Suffering. He has the knowledge that what had to be done with regard to the Noble Truth of the End of Suffering has been completed. That is, the achievement of the Noble Truth of the End of Suffering. He has the knowledge that what had to be done with regard to the Noble Truth of the way leading to the End of Suffering has been completed in terms of virtue, concentration, and wisdom. That is, the development of the Noble Truth of the way leading to the End of Suffering. This is the third phase.

In this way, we have passed through an era where thousands of Arahants lived with the all-encompassing knowledge of the Four Noble Truths.

Inspired Utterances of Arahants

There are accounts mentioned in the Dhamma that those Arahants uttered inspired utterances about this amazing transformation which took place in their lives:

"Birth is destroyed. The holy life has been lived. What had to be done to attain enlightenment has been done. There is nothing more to be done to attain enlightenment."

The Era of a Buddha

The era of a Buddha occurs extremely rarely in the world. During that time, the chance to be born human and to come across the teaching of the Buddha is known as a time of momentous fortune. This moment in a human life is an extremely rare occurrence. Arahants are the only ones that make maximum use of this fruitful moment.

Each discourse of the Buddha contains teachings that solely lead to Arahantship in this very life. There aren't any other hidden meanings within it. Wise people are skillful in understanding that fact. With that knowledge, they place confidence in the Buddha. Furthermore, they strongly believe in the ultimate solution presented by the Buddha. They give the highest priority to realizing it. They abandon the home life and go forth into homelessness and become monks and nuns.

The Buddha's Path

The Buddha's path is a name given for the way leading to Nibbāna, preached by the Buddha.

> Sabba pāpassa akaraṇaṁ
> Kusalassa upasampadā
> Sacitta pariyodapanaṁ
> Etaṁ Buddhāna sāsanaṁ

> "To abstain from all evil, to cultivate the thirty-seven aids to enlightenment, and to cleanse your own mind, this is the teaching of all Buddhas."

Dhammapada, verse 183

Entering the Buddha's Path

Entering the Buddha's path means that you embrace the Three Refuges and receive the full ordination. After that, one is gradually tamed, all the way up to Arahantship. It is because of this that Arahants utter the inspired utterance saying "Kataṁ buddhassa sāsanaṁ" (the Buddha's path has been fully followed).

The Buddha had this unsurpassed, extraordinary ability to guide the disciples who enter the path until Arahantship is reached. There is an occasion in the Middle Length Discourses where the Buddha explains the instructions on taming his disciples to a brāhmin named Gaṅaka Moggallāna in the Gaṅaka Moggallāna Sutta (Majjhima Nikāya 107).

Instructions from the Buddha

"Just as, brāhmin, when a clever horse-trainer obtains a fine thoroughbred horse, he first makes him get used to wearing the bit, and afterwards trains him further, so too when a person comes to the Tathāgata to be tamed, he first disciplines him thus: 'Come monk, be virtuous, restrained with the restraint of the major code of discipline, possess courteous behavior and good conduct, and seeing fear in the slightest fault, train in the precepts you have undertaken.'

Guard Your Sense Faculties

"When, brāhmin, the monk is virtuous... and seeing fear in the slightest fault, trains in the precepts he has undertaken, then the Tathāgata disciplines him further: 'Come, monk, guard the doors of your sense faculties. On seeing a form with the eye, do not grasp at its signs and features. Since, if you were to leave the eye faculty unguarded, evil unwholesome states of desire and anger might invade you, therefore practice the way of its restraint, guard the eye faculty, undertake the restraint of the eye faculty. On hearing a sound with the ear... On smelling an odour with the nose... On tasting a flavour with the tongue... On touching a tangible with the body... On cognizing a mind-object with the mind, do not grasp at its signs and features. Since, if you were to leave the mind faculty unguarded, evil unwholesome states of desire and anger might invade you, therefore practice the way of its restraint, guard the mind faculty, and practice the restraint of the mind faculty.'

Take Meals with Full Awareness

"When, brāhmin, the monk guards the doors of his sense faculties, then the Tathāgata disciplines him further: 'Come, monk, be moderate in eating. Reflecting wisely, you should take food, neither for fun nor for intoxication nor for the sake of physical beauty and attractiveness, but only for the endurance and continuance of this body, for ending painful feelings, and for assisting the holy life, considering: "Thus I shall give up old feelings without making new feelings and I shall be healthy and blameless and shall live in comfort.'

Meditating with Wakefulness

"When, brāhmin, the monk is moderate in eating, then the Tathāgata disciplines him further: 'Come, monk, be devoted to meditation with wakefulness. During the day, while walking back and forth and sitting, clean your mind of states that block it. In the first part of the night, while walking back and forth and sitting, clean your mind of states that block it. In the middle part of the night you should lie down on the right side in the lion's pose with one foot overlapping the other, mindful and fully aware, after noting in your mind the time for wakening up. After rising in the morning, in the third part of the night, while walking back and forth and sitting, clean your mind of states that block it.'

Be Mindful of Your Body Position and Daily Routines

"When, brāhmin, the monk is devoted to wakefulness, then the Tathāgata disciplines him further: 'Come, monk, be possessed of mindfulness and full attentiveness. Act in full awareness when going forward and returning; act in full awareness when looking ahead and looking away; act in full awareness when flexing and stretching your limbs; act in full awareness when wearing your robes and carrying your double robe and bowl; act in full awareness when eating, drinking, consuming food, and tasting; act in full awareness when defecating and urinating; act in full awareness when walking, standing, sitting, falling asleep, waking up, talking, and keeping silent.' (This means that one should not allow unwholesome states to arise)

Live in Seclusion

"When, brāhmin, the monk possesses mindfulness and full awareness, then the Tathāgata disciplines him further: 'Come, monk, spend time in a secluded resting place: the forest, the root of a tree, a mountain, a ravine, a hillside cave, a charnel ground, a jungle thicket, an open space or a heap of straw.'

Give Up the Five Hindrances

"He resorts to a secluded resting place: the forest... a heap of straw. On returning from his alms round, after his meal he sits down, folding his legs crosswise, setting his body straight, and establishing mindfulness on the meditation object. Giving up greed for the world, he lives with a mind free from greed; he purifies his mind from greed. Giving up ill will and hatred, he lives with a mind free from ill will, compassionate for the wellbeing of all living beings; he cleans his mind of ill will and hatred. Giving up sleepiness and drowsiness, he lives free from sleepiness and drowsiness, able to perceive light, mindful and fully aware; he purifies his mind from sleepiness and drowsiness. Giving up restlessness and remorse, he lives without an agitated mind and is peaceful inside; he purifies his mind from restlessness and remorse. Giving up doubt, he lives having gone beyond doubt, without confusion about wholesome states; he purifies his mind from doubt.

Attain Jhānas

"Having thus given up these five hindrances, imperfections of the mind that weaken wisdom, quite secluded from sensual pleasures, secluded from unwholesome states, he enters upon and stays in the first jhāna, which has applied and sustained thought, with rapture and pleasure born of seclusion.

"With the stilling of applied and sustained thought, he enters upon and stays in the second jhāna, which has self-confidence and singleness of mind without applied and sustained thought, with rapture and pleasure born of concentration.

"With the fading away as well of rapture, he lives in equanimity, and mindful and fully aware, still feeling pleasure with the body, he enters upon and stays in the third jhāna, because of which noble ones announce: 'He has a pleasant abiding who has equanimity and is mindful.'

"With the abandoning of pleasure and pain, and with the previous disappearance of joy and grief, he enters upon and stays in the fourth jhāna, which has neither-pain-nor-pleasure and purity of mindfulness due to equanimity.

"This is my instruction, brāhmin, to those monks who are in the higher training, whose minds have not yet attained the goal of Arahantship, who live hoping to achieve the supreme security from bondage.

"But these things lead to both to a pleasant living here and now and to mindfulness and full awareness for those monks who are arahants with taints destroyed, who have lived the holy life, done what had to be done, laid down the burden of defilements, reached the goal gradually, destroyed the things that tie one to existence, and are completely liberated through final knowledge."

In this manner, having developed the knowledge of seeing things as they really are, that monk or nun contemplates all formations as impermanent, suffering, and non-self. Through the realization of the Four Noble Truths, he becomes liberated from suffering.

Marvelous Lives

Now you have learned about the incredible gradual training used by the Buddha to discipline his disciples. The Buddha explained about the noble lives of his enlightened disciples who were fully tamed under that instruction in this way:

"Monks, to whatever extent there are dwelling places of beings, even up to the peak of existence, Arahants are the foremost in the world, Arahants are the Supreme.

Paṭama Arahanta Sutta, SN 22.76

Verses of Enlightened Nuns

Through this sacred book, you will meet the noble nuns who attained enlightenment when the Buddha was alive.

These exalted nuns achieved the essence of the Buddha's path: the liberation through Arahantship and ultimate freedom. The account of their struggle for enlightenment is amazing. It is hard to imagine how they practiced the Dhamma with such extreme energy and determination, even at a risk to their own lives.

Saying "Saṅghaṁ saranaṁ gacchāmi," we go for refuge to this community of noble disciples. How exalted and pure they are! We who are living in the twenty-sixth century of the Buddhist era can be overjoyed simply by recollecting the pure lives of such enlightened disciples.

While you are reading this sacred book, those Arahant nuns might seem to appear in front of you. You will feel like they are conversing with you. You will witness before you the display of the ultimate purity of their hearts. The community of the Buddha's noble disciples is absolutely remarkable and magnificent.

Venerable resident monks in the Mahamewnawa Meditation Monastery, members of the Maha Sangha, and faithful devotees supported me in compiling this sacred book. May they achieve the Supreme bliss of Nibbāna!

May our noble friends, Mr. Dayawamsa Jayakodi and Mrs. Jayakodi, and their staff who aided in of the publishing of this sacred book, also achieve Nibbāna! May you who read this book attain Nibbāna in this Gautama Buddha's path!

Ven. Kiribathgoda Ñānānanda Thero

Mahamewnāwa Meditation Monastery
Vaduwāwa, Yatigaloluwa
Polgahawela
Telephone: 037-2244602

Recollecting the Exalted Qualities
of the Community of Noble Monks and Nuns

Supaṭipanno Bhagavato Sāvaka Saṅgho

The community of noble disciples of the Buddha is dedicated to the path of the eradication of passion, hatred and delusion by the three-fold training of virtue, concentration, and wisdom. Of pure conduct is the community of disciples, of the Blessed One—Supatipanno. I go for refuge and pay homage to the community of disciples!

Ujupaṭipanno Bhagavato Sāvaka Saṅgho

The community of the noble disciples of the Buddha is dedicated to following the straight way called the Noble Eightfold Path. Of upright conduct is the community of disciples of the Blessed One—Ujupaṭipanno. I go for refuge and pay homage to the community of disciples!

Ñāyapaṭipanno Bhagavato Sāvaka Saṅgho

The community of noble disciples of the Buddha is dedicated to the realization of the Four Noble Truths. Of wise conduct is the community of disciples of the Blessed One—Ñāyapaṭipanno. I go for refuge and pay homage to the community of disciples!

Sāmīcipaṭipanno Bhagavato Sāvaka Saṅgho

The community of the noble disciples of the Buddha is dedicated to propagating the pure teachings of the Supremely Enlightened Buddha with utmost respect. Of generous conduct is the community of disciples of the Blessed One—Sāmīcipaṭipanno. I go for refuge and pay homage to the community of disciples!

Yadidam cattāri purisayugāni aṭṭha purisapuggalā esa Bhagavato sāvakasaṅgho

The community of the noble disciples of the Blessed One consists of four pairs of persons:

1. The disciple practicing the path for the attainment of Stream-entry and the Stream-entrant.
2. The disciple practicing the path for the attainment of Once-returning and the Once-returner.
3. The disciple practicing the path for the attainment of Non-returning and the Non-returner.
4. The disciple practicing the path for the attainment of Arahantship and the Arahant.

The community of the noble disciples of the Blessed One consists of the eight kinds of individuals:

1. The disciple practicing the path for the attainment of Stream-entry.
2. The Stream-entrant.
3. The disciple practicing the path for the attainment of Once-returning
4. The Once-returner.
5. The disciple practicing the path for the attainment of Non-returning
6. The Non-returner.
7. The disciple practicing the path for the attainment of Arahantship
8. The Arahant.

I go for refuge and pay homage to the community of disciples of the Blessed One!

Āhuneyyo Bhagavato sāvakasaṅgho

The community of noble disciples of the Buddha is worthy of offerings that are brought from far away, such as robes, alms food, resting places and medicine. I go for refuge and pay homage to the community of disciples of the Blessed One!

Pāhuneyyo Bhagavato sāvakasaṅgho

The community of noble disciples of the Buddha is worthy of hospitality. I go for refuge and pay homage to the community of disciples of the Blessed One!

Dhakkineyyo Bhagavato sāvakasaṅgho

The community of noble disciples of the Buddha is worthy of gifts that are offered by the donors expecting great fruits and results. I go for refuge and pay homage to the community of disciples of the Blessed One!

Añjalikaranīyo Bhagavato sāvakasaṅgho

The community of noble disciples of the Buddha is worthy of reverential salutations by humans and gods. I go for refuge and pay homage to the community of disciples of the Blessed One!

Anuttaraṁ Puññakkhettaṁ lokassā ti

The community of noble disciples of the Buddha is the incomparable field of merit that aids beings to accumulate merit. I go for refuge and pay homage to the community of disciples of the Blessed One!

Sadhu! Sadhu! Sadhu!

Verses of Introduction
Nidāna Gāthā

The Liberated Ones developed their minds through this excellent Dhamma. Listen carefully to the verses uttered by them about their lives. Indeed, these verses are like the roar of cave dwelling lions with strong teeth.

These Enlightened Ones are known by various names and clans. They are endowed with various attainments. They have liberated from all suffering.

They attained ultimate freedom, Nibbāna, through deep penetration by insight. Truly, reflecting on the perfect Dhamma taught by their superb master, the Buddha, these enlightened ones uttered these sweet verses.

Section of Single Verses

The verse of a certain Arahant Nun

1. Nun, you made this robe from a rag cloth. You can live very happily wearing it. You were freed from lust just like leaves that were burnt and shrivelled in a pot.

This verse was said by a certain Arahant Nun.

The verse of Arahant Nun Muttā

2. Muttā, you must be freed from Māra, the evil one, like the moon is freed from Rāhu. You must use your alms food with a mind that has been completely freed from defilements and is without debt.

This verse was said by Arahant Nun Muttā.

The verse of Arahant Nun Puṇṇā

3. Puṇṇā, you must fill your life with noble qualities like the full moon on the Uposatha day. With fulfilled wisdom, split the darkness of ignorance.

This verse was said by Arahant Nun Puṇṇā.

The verse of Arahant Nun Tissā

4. Tissā, be trained in the training of virtue, concentration and wisdom. Don't miss this very rare opportunity! Liberate yourself from all fetters. Live without taints in the world.

This verse was said by Arahant Nun Tissā.

The verse of Arahant Nun Tissā

5. Tissā, practice the Dhamma. Don't miss this very rare opportunity! Those who have missed this excellent opportunity suffer when they fall into hell.

This verse was said by Arahant Nun Tissā.

The verse of Arahant Nun Dhīrā

6. Dhīrā, you should experience Nibbāna, the end of suffering. The absence of unwholesome perceptions is peaceful. Yes, liberate yourself from these defilements and gain unsurpassed Nibbāna.

This verse was said by Arahant Nun Dhīrā.

The verse of Arahant Nun Vīrā

7. Nun, with strong effort develop the faculties of faith, energy, mindfulness, concentration and wisdom. Keep on practicing the Dhamma. Having defeated Māra, the evil one, and his army, bear your last body.

This verse was said by Arahant Nun Vīrā.

The verse of Arahant Nun Mittā

8. Mittā, you became a nun out of faith. Delight in the association of noble friends. Develop wholesome qualities for the attainment of Arahantship.

This verse was said by Arahant Nun Mittā.

The verse of Arahant Nun Bhadrā

9. Bhadrā, you became a nun out of faith. Therefore you must delight in this excellent, beautiful Dhamma. Develop wholesome qualities for the attainment of Arahantship.

This verse was said by Arahant Nun Bhadrā.

The verse of Arahant Nun Upasamā

10. Upasamā, it is very hard to cross over the realm of Māra, the evil one. However you should cross over the flood of saṁsāra. Defeat Māra, the evil one, and his army. Bear your last body.

This verse was said by Arahant Nun Upasamā.

The verse of Arahant Nun Muttā

11. It is good that I am released from everything. I am well released from the three crooked things: the mortar, pestle, and my husband. I am also released from the cycle of birth and death along with craving that leads to rebirth.

This verse was said by Arahant Nun Muttā.

The verse of Arahant Nun Dhammadinnā

12. The only desire in my mind was to attain Nibbāna. I wasn't distracted by any other desires. I contacted Nibbāna with my mind. One whose mind is not attached to sensual pleasures is called one heading up-stream.

This verse was said by Arahant Nun Dhammadinnā.

The verse of Arahant Nun Visākhā

13. If you don't want to do something you will regret later, then follow the Buddha's instructions. Wash your feet quickly and sit down to meditate!

This verse was said by Arahant Nun Visākhā.

The verse of Arahant Nun Sumanā

14. Understand the four great elements as suffering and do not be born again in this saṁsāra. Discarding the desire for existence, live with a still mind.

This verse was said by Arahant Nun Sumanā.

The verse of Arahant Nun Uttarā

15. I was restrained in my body, speech and mind. I plucked out craving from its root. I became cool and quenched.

This verse was said by Arahant Nun Uttarā.

The verse of Arahant Nun Sumanā, who became a nun when she was old.

16. Old lady, sleep peacefully in the robe that you sewed from rag cloths. Your lust has ceased. Therefore, become cool and quenched.

This verse was said by Arahant Nun Sumanā, who became a nun when she was old.

The verse of Arahant Dhammā

17. My body was so weak. I went on my alms round using a walking stick, with my hand and legs shaking. That day, when I fell down, my mind focused on the danger of this body and I was released from all defilements.

This verse was said by Arahant Nun Dhammā.

The verse of Arahant Saṅghā

18. I gave up my beloved sons and daughters, my cattle and animals and my house. I became a nun. Eventually, I also gave up lust and hatred. Discarding ignorance, and plucking out craving from its root, I became stilled and quenched.

This verse was said by Arahant Nun Saṅghā.

Section of Two Verses

The verses of Arahant Nun Gorgeous Nandā

19. Nandā, see carefully this disgusting body that is diseased, impure, rotten, oozing, and filthy. With a well-concentrated mind, develop the meditation on the impurities of the body.

20. Develop insight meditation which is free from signs of defilements. Uproot the conceit in the mind. Abandoning conceit with full understanding, live in peace.

These verses were said by Arahant Nun Gorgeous Nandā.

The verses of Arahant Nun Jentā

21. As the way leading to Nibbāna, these seven aids for enlightenment were taught by the Supreme Buddha. I have developed all of them.

22. I have indeed seen the Blessed One through the Dhamma. This is my final body. Journeying on from birth to birth has ended. There is no longer any existence for me.

These verses were said by Arahant Nun Jentā.

The verses of Arahant Nun Sumangalamātā

23. You are released from everything. Yes, you are well released. It is good that you are released from the pestle. My husband had no shame whatsoever. I disliked even his umbrella. My pots even stank badly.

24. I destroyed lust and hate with a sizzle and pop. Now, when I go up to the foot of a tree, I think, "Oh, what a wonderful happiness." I meditate with immense happiness.

These verses were said by Arahant Nun Sumangalamātā

The verses of Arahant Nun Aḍḍhakāsī

25. My wage for being a prostitute was set equal to half the tax revenue of the province of Kāsi. The people of the province fixed that price and made me their prostitute.

26. But now, with full understanding I have become disenchanted with my body. I have become dispassionate. I will never run through the journeying-on from birth to birth again. I have attained the Triple Knowledge and completed the training of the Buddha.

These verses were said by Arahant Nun Aḍḍhakāsī.

The verses of Arahant Nun Cittā

27. I am very thin, sick and weak. But still, leaning on a stick, I climbed the Mountain Gijjhakūṭa.

28. I put my bowl aside, turning it upside down, and put my double robe aside as well. I sat on a rock. I tore apart the dark mass of ignorance.

These verses were said by Arahant Nun Cittā.

The verses of Arahant Nun Mettikā

29. I was in great pain, weak, with my youth gone. But still, leaning on a stick I climbed the Mountain Gijjhakūṭa.

30. I put my bowl aside, turning it upside down, and put my double robe aside as well. I sat on a rock. There, my mind was completely released from taints. I have attained the Triple Knowledge and completed the Buddha's training.

These verses were said by Arahant Nun Mettikā.

The verses of Arahant Nun Mettā

31. Previously, I observed uposatha, keeping eight precepts. My wish was to be reborn in heaven.

32. But now I eat a single meal. I live with a shaved head, a bowl, and robes. I have removed all defilements from my heart. Now, I no longer wish for a rebirth in heaven.

These verses were said by Arahant Nun Mettā.

The verses of Arahant Nun Abhayamātā

33. Mother, from the soles of the feet upwards, from the head and hair downwards, reflect on this impure, evil smelling body.

34. [According to the advice of my son Abhaya,] I wisely reflected on this body. I rooted out all desire. I have cut out the burning fever of defilements. Now I have become cool and quenched.

These verses were said by Arahant Nun Abhayamātā.

The verses of Arahant Nun Abhayā

35. Abhayā, ordinary people are attached to the body. But the reality is the body is fragile. Having wisely reflected on this fact with clear mindfulness, I will discard this body.

36. I used this life full of pain only for practicing the Dhamma diligently. Craving has been destroyed. I have attained Nibbāna and completed the Buddha's training.

These verses were said by Arahant Nun Abhayā.

The verses of Arahant Nun Sāmā

37. Previously, I was unable to gain any unification of mind. I had no control over my mind. I left the monastery four or five times a day.

38. But finally, when the eighth night passed since I became a nun, I completely rooted out craving. I took the Dhamma practice seriously because of the many pains in this life. Craving has been destroyed. I have attained Nibbāna and completed the Buddha's training.

These verses were said by Arahant Nun Sāmā.

Section of Three Verses

The verses of Arahant Nun Sāmā

39. Twenty-five years have passed since I became a nun. During this period my mind has not achieved any meditative happiness at all.

40. Without self-mastery over the mind, without any unification of the mind, and while recollecting the instructions of the Buddha, I experienced a sense of urgency.

41. I took the Dhamma practice seriously because of the many pains in this life. Craving has been destroyed. I have attained Nibbāna and completed the Buddha's training. Today is the seventh day since my craving has dried up.

These verses were said by Arahant Nun Sāmā.

The verses of Arahant Nun Uttamā

42. Previously, I didn't have any unification of mind. I didn't have any control over it. I would leave the monastery four or five times a day.

43. There was a certain nun in whom I had confidence. I approached her and she taught me the Dhamma about aggregates, elements and sense bases.

44. As I listened attentively to what she taught me, my mind was overjoyed. I sat in the same cross legged position for seven days. On the eighth day, having torn apart the dark mass of ignorance, I stretched out my legs.

These verses were said by Arahant Nun Uttamā.

The verses of Arahant Nun Uttamā

45. The seven aids for enlightenment were taught by the Buddha. I have developed all of them.

46. I developed the attainment of emptiness and the attainment of signlessness as I wished. Now I am a true daughter of the Buddha, born from the Blessed One's heart. I always live delighting in Nibbāna.

47. All divine and human sensual pleasures have been completely cut off. Journeying on from birth to birth has been completely ended. There is no existence for me anymore.

These verses were said by Arahant Nun Uttamā.

The verses of Arahant Nun Dantikā

48. Going out from my daytime resting place on Mount Gijjhakūṭa, on the riverbank I saw an elephant just after a bath.

49. A man, using a hook, demanded the elephant stretch out his foot. The elephant stretched out its foot and the man climbed up on its back.

50. This elephant was previously untamed. But later it was tamed by people. I was watching how the elephant was taken under control. This incident struck my heart deeply. Having gone to the forest, I concentrated and tamed my mind.

These verses were said by Arahant Nun Dantikā.

The verses of Arahant Nun Ubbirī

51. [The Buddha:] In the forest, Ubbiri, you are sobbing and calling out, "Oh my daughter, Jīva!" Did you know that eighty-four thousand people were burnt in this cemetery, all whose name was Jīva? Which of them do you grieve for?

52. When I heard this, I plucked out the dart of sorrow I had for my daughter. It was hard to see while it was stuck in my heart.

53. Today I live with the dart plucked out and with craving abandoned. My mind is fully quenched. I took the Supreme Buddha, Supreme Dhamma, and the Supreme Saṅgha as my refuge.

These verses were said by Arahant Nun Ubbirī.

The verses of Arahant Nun Sukkā

54. This nun Sukkā is teaching the Buddha's Dhamma. What has happened to these people in the city of Rājagaha? If they don't come to hear her, it is as though they are drunk and asleep.

55. But wise people don't miss out on this Dhamma. This Dhamma's nature is very sweet. It is juicy with the flavour of wholesome qualities. One should listen to this Dhamma as a traveller in a desert drinks rain water.

56. This nun Sukkā has wholesome qualities. She is lust free and concentrated. She has defeated Māra and his army. She bears her final body.

These verses were said by Arahant Nun Sukkā.

The verses of Arahant Nun Selā

57. [Māra:] There is nothing called Nibbāna in this world. So what are you doing here in seclusion? Go and enjoy sensual pleasures. Don't regret it later!

58. [Nun Selā:] Hey Māra! Sensual pleasures are like poisoned swords. The five aggregates are like slabs of meat. What you call enjoyment is boring to me.

59. I got rid of desire for everything. I tore apart the dark mass of ignorance. Māra, know that you are defeated.

These verses were said by Arahant Nun Selā.

The verses of Arahant Nun Somā

60. [Māra:] Arahantship is very hard to attain. It is attained by Great Buddhas and seers. How could such a thing be realized by a woman with a two-finger intelligence?

61. [Nun Somā:] Hey Māra! If the mind is well-concentrated, what failure will this woman's state bring? When wisdom is achieved with clear insight, what failure will this woman's state bring?

62. I got rid of all desire for everything. I tore apart the dark mass of ignorance. Māra, know that you are defeated.

These verses were said by Arahant Nun Somā.

Section of Four Verses

The verses of Arahant Nun Bhaddā Kāpilānī

63. The Great Arahant Kassapa is the son, the heir, of the Buddha. With a well-concentrated mind, he sees the past lives of beings and sees heaven and hell with his divine eye.

64. Having attained the destruction of rebirth, he has become a liberated one. Since he achieved the Triple Knowledge, he is a true Brāhmin.

65. Bhaddā Kāpilānī is same as the Great Arahant Kassapa. She also has achieved the Triple Knowledge. Having defeated Māra and his army, she now bears her final body.

66. We were both ordained having realized the disadvantages of cycle of rebirths. We were well tamed and liberated. We have become cool and quenched.

These verses were said by Arahant Nun Bhaddā Kāpilānī.

Section of Five Verses

The verses of a certain Arahant Nun

67. Twenty-five years have passed since I became a nun. During this whole time, I could not obtain unification of mind, not even for the duration of a finger snap.

68. Not having obtained any unification of mind I suffered a lot from lust for sensual pleasures. Finally, weeping, with my hands on my head, I went from monastery to monastery.

69. There was a very skillful nun in whom I had confidence. I approached her and she taught me the Dhamma about aggregates, elements, and sense bases.

70. I took to heart the Dhamma that was taught to me by that skillful nun. I sat down in a quiet place. Now I have the ability to recollect my previous lives. I have also purified my divine eye.

71. I also have the ability to read others' minds and have purified the divine eye. I am skilled in displaying miracles of supernatural powers. Having attained the destruction of taints, I became liberated. I have attained all of these superior knowledges and have completed the training of the Buddha.

These verses were said by a certain Arahant Nun.

The verses of Arahant Nun Vimalā

72. In the past, I was extremely beautiful and fit. I was intoxicated by all the luxurious comforts around me. I was self-absorbed and conceited. I despised other women.

73. Back then I decorated my body with beautiful ornaments. Having dressed in a way that foolish people praise, I would wait at the corner of the street like a deer hunter having placed a trap.

74. I used to wear seductive clothing. I did various sorts of tricks to attract men. Foolish men fell easily under my spell, and I lured them towards me.

75. But now as a nun with a shaved head, wearing robes, I live depending on food from my alms round. I spend my time meditating under trees. My mind is well-concentrated.

76. I have cut off all ties that lead to rebirth as a human or a god. I have destroyed all taints. I have become cool and quenched.

These verses were said by Arahant Nun Vimalā.

The verses of Arahant Nun Sīhā

77. Previously, in the beginning of my life as a nun, I thought in the wrong way. I was overwhelmed by desire for sensual pleasures. My mind was distracted and I failed to control it.

78. Because my mind was preoccupied with signs of attractiveness, I was obsessed with defilements. Being under the influence of lustful thoughts, I did not obtain any unification of mind.

79. Back then I was very thin, pale, and shabby. I suffered in that life for seven years. Suffering from defilements, I did not achieve any spiritual happiness from the nun-life.

80. Finally, taking a rope, I went into the forest thinking "It is better to hang myself than to go back to the low lay life."

81. I made a strong noose and tied it to a branch of a tree. I put the noose around my neck. It was then that my mind was released completely from all defilements.

These verses were said by Arahant Nun Sīhā.

The verses of Arahant Nun Nandā

82. Nandā, see wisely this disgusting body that is diseased, impure, rotten, oozing, and filthy. Develop the meditation on the impurities of this body with a well-concentrated mind.

83. Both this body and a dead body are the same. What is in the dead body is also in this body. This body smells bad and oozes with filth. But foolish people are very attached to the body.

84. I investigated the foul nature of this body throughout the whole day. I broke through to the true nature of this body with my own developed wisdom.

85. As the result of my diligent, wise consideration, I realized the true nature of this internal body and the bodies of others.

86. I became disenchanted with this body and was inwardly dispassionate. Working hard, I escaped from all defilements. I have become stilled and quenched.

These verses were said by Arahant Nun Nandā.

The verses of Arahant Nun Nanduttarā

87. I used to worship the fire god, the moon god, and the sun god. Having gone to rivers, I would plunge into the water to wash away my sins.

88. I practiced various types of vows. I shaved half my head. I slept on the ground. I ate nothing at night.

89. When I would come home, I would take a bath. Then I would decorate myself with ornaments. Being intoxicated with sensual desires, I comforted my body.

90. But now I have gained confidence in the Buddha's training. I became a nun. When I understood the true nature of this body, sensual desires were completely rooted out.

91. I have cut off all existences, wishes and longings. Detached from all defilements, I have attained the supreme peace of mind.

These verses were said by Arahant Nun Nanduttarā.

The verses of Arahant Nun Mittakālī

92. Having given up the home life, I truly became a nun through faith. But then I became caught up in gain and honor. I wandered here and there longing only for those things.

93. I missed the highest good and went after the lowest things. I didn't have any idea to achieve spiritual goals.

94. One day when I was in my little hut, a shocking disturbance suddenly arose in me. "Because I am caught up in craving, I have entered the wrong road!

95. I have a very short time left to live. Old age and sickness are rolling in on me. Eventually, damaged by old age this body will fall apart. There is no time for me to be negligent."

96. I started to investigate wisely the arising and the passing away of the five aggregates of clinging as they really are. As a result, my mind was completely released from all defilements. The Buddha's path has been fully followed by me.

These verses were said by Arahant Nun Mittakālī.

The verses of Arahant Nun Sakulā

97. When I lived at home, I learned the perfect Dhamma from a monk. Through that Dhamma, I attained the undefiled, deathless Nibbāna.

98. I gave up my son, daughter, money, and property. Having shaved off my hair, I became a nun.

99. I started the practice while I was a trainee. I progressively eliminated lust and hate along with other defilements.

100. Eventually I received the higher ordination. I recollected my past lives and purified the divine eye which is developed by pure-minded noble ones.

101. I realized the selfless nature of all formations that have arisen with a cause and are liable to destruction. I eliminated all taints. I have become cool and quenched.

These verses were said by Arahant Nun Sakulā.

The verses of Arahant Nun Soṇā

102. Because of having this body, I had to give birth to ten children. This made me very weak and aged. Finally, I approached a certain nun.

103. She taught me the Dhamma about aggregates, elements and sense bases. I took to heart the Dhamma taught by that nun. Shaving off my hair, I became a nun.

104. I purified the divine eye while I was a trainee and achieved the knowledge to see my past lives.

105. With a well-concentrated mind I developed insight. I became liberated. I have become quenched without clinging.

106. Since I comprehended the five aggregates of clinging, now they stand with roots cut off. Hey! Inferior old age, shame on you! Now there is no more rebirth for me.

These verses were said by Arahant Nun Soṇā.

The verses of Arahant Nun Bhaddā Kuṇḍalakesā

107. I used to lead a very strange life. I pulled out my hair with my hand. I didn't brush my teeth. I wore only one piece of cloth. Back then I thought that wrong deeds were correct deeds and correct deeds were wrong deeds.

108. One day I saw the stainless Buddha surrounded by a community of monks climbing down from the Mount Gijjhakūṭa in the evening. I went to the presence of the Supreme Buddha.

109. Kneeling down and placing my hands together, I worshiped the Great Buddha. The Buddha said to me: "Come here Bhaddā." That was my higher ordination.

110. Previously I used to wander over the provinces of Aṅga, Magadha, Vajjī, Kāsi, and Kosala. Even now I wander over there but as one who is debt free. It has been fifty years since I started eating food as a liberated nun.

111. This wise male, lay disciple collected much merit. You offered the robe to the nun Bhaddhā who was freed from all defilements.

These verses were said by Arahant Nun Bhaddā Kuṇḍalakesā.

The verses of Arahant Nun Patācārā

112. When working the fields with plows, sewing seeds in the earth, and caring for wives and children, people generate wealth.

113. I am not lazy or arrogant. I possess a virtuous life and practice the Buddha's training. So why am I not able to achieve Nibbāna?

114. I poured water on my feet to wash them. I saw that water flow down from high to low.

115. I concentrated my mind very well on that incident. My mind became tamed like the best type of horse. Then I took the lamp and entered my hut.

116. With the light of the lamp I found the bed and sat on it. To put out the flame, I pulled down the wick of the oil lamp. That was the moment my mind was liberated from all defilements, just like the extinguishing of an oil lamp.

These verses were said by Arahant Nun Patācārā.

The verses of thirty Arahant Nuns

117. Taking pestles, people grind grains. Taking care of their families, they find wealth.

118. Practice the Buddha's training. Having practiced it, one does not regret. Wash your feet quickly and sit down quietly. Develop unification of mind and complete the Buddha's path.

119. The Nun Patācarā instructed the nuns in this way. Those nuns took that instruction to their hearts. They washed their feet, and sat down quietly. They developed unification of the mind and completed the Buddha's path.

120. In the first watch of the night, they recollected their past lives. In the middle watch of the night they purified the divine eye. In the last watch of the night they tore apart the dark mass of ignorance.

121. Those nuns worshiped the feet of nun Patācarā saying, "We have succeeded following your instruction. We live honoring you like the Tāvatimsa Gods honoring the God Sakka after winning the battle against Asurās. We have achieved the Triple Knowledge and live without taints."

These verses were said by thirty Arahant Nuns.

The verses of Arahant Nun Candā

122. Formerly, as a widow without children, I suffered a lot. Without friends and relations, I did not obtain food or clothing.

123. Taking a clay bowl and a stick, I went begging from house to house. Suffering from the cold and heat, I wandered for seven years.

124. One day, I saw the nun Patācarā obtaining plenty of food and drink. I approached her and said, "Please ordain me as a nun."

125. The nun Patācarā had pity on me. She ordained me. Then she instructed me and urged me towards the highest goal.

126. I took her instruction to heart and followed it. Her instruction was not in vain. Now I also have achieved the Triple Knowledge and live without taints.

These verses were said by Arahant Nun Candā.

Section of Six Verses

The verses of five hundred Arahant Nuns

127. We don't know where he came from. We don't know where he goes to. That being the case, for whom do you lament, crying, "my son"?

128. But you do not grieve for a person who's coming and going. The journey of saṁsāra is unknown to you. You realize that this is the nature of all beings.

129. Uninvited a person comes into this world, without permission that person leaves this world. Surely having come from a certain world and having lived here for some time, that person goes to another world. Having passed away from there, that person moves on to yet another world.

130. That dead person, having lived here in the form of a human, departed. In whatever way he comes into this world, he departs in the same way. What is there to cry about in that?

131. I was truly in pain over the death of my son. That nun plucked out the vicious dart of sorrow out of my heart.

132. Today, my dart is plucked out. I am withdrawn from craving and am totally quenched. I am well established in the refuge of the Supreme Buddha, Dhamma, and Saṅgha.

These verses were said by five hundred Arahant Nuns.

The verses of Arahant Nun Vāseṭṭhi

133. I couldn't bear the pain of my son's death. I went crazy and lost my mindfulness. I didn't even wear clothes. With a messy head of hair, I wandered here and there.

134. I lived on heaps of rubbish in the streets, in cemeteries, and on highways. I wandered like this for three years, suffering from hunger and thirst.

135. One day, I saw the Supreme Buddha entering the city of Mithilā. I saw the Supremely Enlightened Buddha, the tamer of the untamed beings and the one who has no fear at all.

136. With that sight, I regained my mind and came to my senses. I went to the Buddha and worshiped him. Gautama Supreme Buddha showed pity on me and preached the Dhamma to me.

137. Having heard the excellent Dhamma, I became a nun. Following the Supreme Teacher's instruction, I attained the bliss of Nibbāna.

138. All grief has been cut out and completely eliminated. I have comprehended all those objects that arise from grief.

These verses were said by Arahant Nun Vāseṭṭhi.

The verses of Arahant Nun Khemā

139. [Māra:] Dear Khemā, you are still young and beautiful. I am also young and in my prime. Come, let us enjoy sensual pleasures and delight in sweet music.

140. [Nun Khemā:] Hey Māra, I am disgusted and ashamed of this foul body that is subject to disease and destruction. I have rooted out craving for sensual pleasures.

141. Sensual pleasures are like swords smeared with poison. The five aggregates of clinging are like piles of flesh. What you call delight in sensual pleasures is now non-delight for me.

142. I have gotten rid of craving for everything. I tore apart the dark mass of ignorance. That is how you should understand me. Māra, in this case you are defeated.

143. Not knowing reality, foolish people revere superstitions and worship the fire in the forest searching for purity.

144. But I worship the Supremely Enlightened Buddha, the best of men. Following the great teacher's instruction, I have been completely released from all suffering.

These verses were said by Arahant Nun Khemā.

The verses of Arahant Nun Sujātā

145. One day I was well dressed and decorated with jewelry. I was wearing flower garlands. My body was smeared with sandalwood cream. I was surrounded by my female attendants.

146. Taking an abundance of food, drinks, sweets and snacks I went to the park to have fun.

147. Having enjoyed playing there, on my way home, I visited the Añjana Forest Monastery in Sāketa.

148. There I saw the Supreme Buddha shining like the brightest lamp that illuminates all three worlds. I approached the Great Teacher and worshiped him. Out of compassion for me, the Supreme Buddha, the one with eyes of Dhamma, taught me the excellent teaching.

149. The Buddha is a great seer. Having heard the Supreme Dhamma, I realized the Four Noble Truths. Sitting on that very seat, I attained the lust free state, Nibbāna.

150. Thus, knowing the true Dhamma, I became a Nun. I attained the Triple Knowledge. The Supreme Buddha's training is never in vain.

Theses verses were said by Arahant Nun Sujātā.

The verses of Arahant Nun Anupamā

151. I was born into an upper class family that had great comforts and wealth. I was extremely beautiful. I was the daughter of Megha, a very rich merchant.

152. Many princes and wealthy merchants desired me. They sent my father messengers saying, "Let me marry your daughter Anupamā.

153. "If you tell us how much your daughter Anupamā weighs, we will give you eight times her weight in gold and jewels."

154. But I saw the Enlightened Buddha who was incomparable and supreme in the world. I paid homage to my great teacher's sacred feet and sat down.

155. Out of compassion for me, Gautama Supreme Buddha taught me the excellent Dhamma. Seated on that very spot, I attained the fruit of non-returning.

156. Then I cut off my hair and became a nun. Today is the seventh night since my craving dried up.

These verses were said by Arahant Nun Anupamā.

The verses of Arahant Nun Mahā Pajāpatī Gotamī

157. The Buddha, the Great Hero, and the best of all beings, I pay my homage to you. It was you who released me and many other people from the suffering of cycle of rebirths.

158. I understood suffering; eradicated craving, the cause of suffering; developed the Noble Eightfold Path and attained Nibbāna, the cessation of suffering.

159. Not knowing the true nature of life, as a helpless being journeying on saṁsāra, at different times I was your mother, son, father, brother and grandmother.

160. I have indeed seen the Blessed One through the Dhamma. I am bearing my final body. Journeying on from birth to birth has been eliminated. There is no more rebirth for me.

161. Look at the monks, the harmonious disciples of the Buddha putting forth energy, giving the Dhamma practice top priority

with strong effort. Rejoicing in their effort is the true Buddha vandana.

162. Truly Queen Māyā gave birth to Gautama Supreme Buddha for the well-being of many. That is indeed how the mass of suffering of those beings who are struck by sickness and death is thrust away.

These verses were said by Arahant Nun Mahā Pajāpatī Gotamī.

The verses of Arahant Nun Guttā

163. Guttā, having given up your dear children and wealth, you became a nun with a noble wish. Therefore you should work towards that wish only. Don't get tricked by your mind!

164. These beings get tricked by the mind, and then they live delighting in Māra's objects. They don't see the true nature of this life. As a result they run on through the journey of saṁsāra for numerous rebirths.

165. There are five fetters: sensual desire, ill will, identity view, clinging to wrong practices, and doubt.

166. After abandoning these five fetters, that nun will never return to rebirth in this sensual existence again.

167. Abandon the fetters of the desire for form, the desire for formless, conceit, restlessness and ignorance, and put an end to all suffering.

168. Annihilating journeying-on from birth to birth, comprehending repeated existence fully, and eradicating craving in this very life, you will become still.

These verses were said by Arahant Nun Guttā.

The verses of Arahant Nun Vijayā

169. Previously being unable to control my mind, I didn't have any unification of mind. I left the monastery four or five times a day.

170. Finally I approached the Nun Khemā. I questioned respectfully and learned the Dhamma from her. She taught me the Dhamma about aggregates, elements and sense bases.

171. She taught me the Four Noble Truths, The Five Spiritual Faculties, the Five Spiritual Powers, the Seven Enlightenment Factors and the Noble Eightfold Path leading to Supreme Nibbāna.

172. Having learned the Dhamma from her, I followed her exact instructions. In the first watch of the night, I gained the knowledge of recollecting my past lives.

173. In the middle watch of the night, I purified the divine eye. In the last watch of the night I tore apart the dark mass of ignorance.

174. I dwelled filling my whole body with joy and happiness. Having torn apart the dark mass of ignorance, on the seventh day, I stretched out my feet.

These verses were said by Arahant Nun Vijayā.

Section of Seven Verses

The verses of Arahant Nun Uttarā

175. Taking pestles, people grind grains. Taking care of their families, they find wealth.

176. Practice the Buddha's training; having practiced it, one does not regret anything. Wash your feet quickly and sit down quietly.

177. With a well-concentrated, unified mind, investigate wisely that all conditioned things are selfless and not belonging to self.

178. I took to my heart the nun Patācārā's instruction. I washed my feet, and sat down quietly.

179. In this first watch of the night, I gained the knowledge of recollecting my past lives. In the middle watch of the night, I purified the divine eye.

180. In the last watch of the night, I tore apart the dark mass of ignorance. That morning I arose with these Triple Knowledges. I have taken your advice.

181. I live honoring you like the Tāvatiṁsa Gods honor the God Sakka after winning the battle against Asurās. I have achieved the Triple Knowledge and live without taints.

These verses were said by Arahant Nun Uttarā.

The verses of Arahant Nun Cālā

182. Having established clear mindfulness, the nun lives with developed spiritual faculties. Her life is established in the peace that comes from stilling all formations. She has achieved the peace of stilling all formations, Nibbāna.

183. [Māra:] For whose sake did you shave your head? You seem like a nun, but why don't you be a female wanderer instead? Why are you being so foolish practicing as a nun?

184. [Nun Cālā:] Hey Māra! Female wanderers are found outside the Buddha's training. They're entangled in various false views. They don't know this true Dhamma. They are not skilled in knowing this true Dhamma.

185. But the incomparable sage who was born to the Sākyan clan is called the Supreme Buddha. He taught me the true Dhamma which leads to the overcoming of all false views.

186. That true Dhamma is about suffering, the arising of suffering, the overcoming of suffering, and the Noble Eightfold Path leading to the stilling of suffering.

187. Having heard my Great Teacher's Dhamma, I delightfully practiced the Buddha's training. I have achieved the Triple Knowledge and completed the Buddha's training.

188. I have gotten rid of desire for everything. I tore apart the dark mass of ignorance. Māra, know that you are defeated.

These verses were said by Arahant Nun Cālā.

The verses of Arahant Nun Upacālā

189. That nun lives with clear mindfulness and with eyes of Dhamma. She has developed Spiritual Faculties. As a result of the association with noble people, she has achieved peaceful Nibbāna.

190. [Māra:] Why don't you like to be reborn? When you are born you enjoy sensual pleasures. Delight in sensual pleasures and enjoy them. Don't have regret later.

191. [Nun Upacālā:] Hey Māra! There is always death for the person who is born: There is the breaking of hands and feet, slaughtering, and various disasters; defilements arise for him. It is the person who is born who falls into suffering.

192. The unconquered Supreme Buddha who was born in the Sākyan clan lives in this world. He taught me the Supreme Dhamma that leads to the complete overcoming of birth.

193. That true Dhamma is about suffering, the arising of suffering, the overcoming of suffering, and the Noble Eightfold Path leading to the stilling of suffering.

194. Having heard my Great Teacher's Dhamma, I delightfully practiced the Buddha's training. I have achieved the Triple Knowledge and completed the Buddha's training.

195. I have gotten rid of desire for everything. I tore apart the dark mass of ignorance. Māra, know that you are defeated.

These verses were said by Arahant Nun Upacālā.

Section of Eight Verses

The verses of Arahant Nun Sisūpacālā

196. That nun is very virtuous, her senses are well controlled. She obtained the taste of Nibbāna which has a sweet flavour.

197. [Māra:] There are deities in the heavens of Tāvatiṃsa, Yāma, Tusita, Previously, you lived in those heavens. Focus your mind to be reborn there.

198-9. [Nun Sisūpacālā:] Hey Māra! Those deities in the heavens of Tāvatiṃsa, Yāma, Tusita, Nimmānarati and Paranimmita Vasa-vatti wander again and again from existence to existence, being caught up in the five aggregates of clinging. They can't go beyond these five aggregates of clinging. They continually wander in this journey of birth and death.

200. Every world is ablaze with defilements. Every world is continuously burning with defilements. Every world is covered with the burning flames of defilements. Every world is shaken by defilements.

201. But the Supreme Buddha is unshaken and incomparable. Noble people associate with him, not ordinary people. The Supreme Buddha taught me the Dhamma. That Dhamma always resonates in my mind.

202. Having heard my Great Teacher's Dhamma, I delightfully practiced the Buddha's training. I have achieved the Triple Knowledge and completed the Buddha's training.

203. I got rid of desire for everything. I tore apart the dark mass of ignorance. Māra, know that you are defeated.

These verses were said by Arahant Nun Sisūpacālā.

Section of Nine Verses

The verses of Arahant Nun Vaḍḍhamātā

204. [Vaḍḍhamātā:] Son Vaḍḍha, may a forest of defilements not grow for you in this world! Son, do not be an owner of suffering again and again.

205. Vaḍḍha, the sages who have eradicated defilements and doubts live in peace. They are well tamed and cooled.

206. Vaḍḍha, you too should follow the path which was followed by those seers. Achieve the realization of the Dhamma. Train to put an end to suffering.

207. [Son Vaḍḍha:] Mother, you are teaching me the Dhamma with strong confidence. My dear mother, indeed a forest of defilements is not found in you.

208. [Vaḍḍhamātā:] Vaḍḍha, I don't even have a minute or trifling amount of craving for any formations whether they are low, high, or middle.

209. I meditated diligently. All my taints have been annihilated. I have achieved the Triple Knowledge and completed the Buddha's training.

210. [Son Vaḍḍha:] Truly my mother has uttered noble words. She has sympathetically instructed me to reach the excellent goal.

211. I listened to my mother's words and diligently reflected on them. I generated a sense of urgency to realize Nibbāna.

212. I strived very hard both day and night. I practiced the Dhamma giving it top priority. I attained the Supreme Bliss of Nibbāna.

These verses were said by Arahant Nun Vaḍḍhamātā.

Section of Eleven Verses

The Verses of Arahant Nun Kisāgotamī

213. Associating with noble friends has been praised by the Great Sage, the Buddha, for the well-being of the world. Through the association of noble friends, even a fool becomes wise.

214. One should associate with wise, noble people. It is through this association that one's wisdom is increased. The one who associates with wise, noble people is liberated from all suffering.

215. The one who associates with wise, noble people comprehends the four noble truths: suffering, the arising of suffering, the cessation of suffering, and the Noble Eightfold Path.

216. The Great Teacher, the incomparable tamer of people, said that the life of a woman is painful. It is truly painful to be a co-wife under one husband. Because of pain some women only give birth once.

217. During labour, some women slit their throats because of unbearable pain. These suffering women take poison to escape pain and die. In some miscarriages both the mother and baby die.

218. When I was ready to give birth, I left to go see my parents. But before I reached their house, I gave birth along the way. I also saw my husband lying dead in the forest.

219. My life was miserable. I witnessed the death of my two sons and my husband. I saw the funeral pyre on which the bodies of my mother, father and sister were being burnt.

220. [The Buddha:] Miserable woman, with family and wealth destroyed, you have suffered immeasurable pain. You have shed tears for thousands of births in this saṁsāra.

221. Wandering in this cycle, I have lived in cemeteries, I have eaten the flesh of my own children, my families have been destroyed, I have been disgraced by everyone. My husbands died in accidents, but in this life I achieved the deathless, Nibbāna, the ultimate freedom.

222. I developed the Noble Eightfold Path leading to deathlessness. I achieved ultimate freedom. I experienced all these attainments through the mirror of the Dhamma.

223. I have cut out the dart of sorrow. I have lowered the heavy load of defilements. What had to be done to end suffering has been done. These were said by the enlightened Nun Kisāgotamī, who has a fully liberated mind.

These verses were said by Arahant Nun Kisāgotamī.

Section of Twelve Verses

The verses of Arahant Nun Uppalavaṇṇā

224. The two of us, my mother and I, were co-wives of the same husband. This situation was shocking to me, unusual, and hair-raising.

225. A curse on sensual pleasures. They are impure, foul smelling, and cause many troubles. Due to these sensual pleasures a mother and her daughter had to become co-wives of the same husband.

226. I saw the danger of sensual pleasures. I understood the withdrawal from sensual pleasures as a fearless protection. Having abandoned the home life and entered homelessness, I became a nun in the city of Rājagaha.

227. Now I have achieved the knowledge to recollect my past lives. My divine eye and divine ear are purified. I also have the ability to read others' minds.

228. I have achieved the psychic powers too. I attained enlightenment achieving the six supernormal knowledges. The Buddha's path has been fully followed by me.

229. I created a four-horse chariot using my psychic powers and rode to the Buddha, the one who has an unshaken mind. I worshiped the sacred feet of the glorious protector of the world.

230. [Māra:] Oh, you are sitting alone at the foot of this sāla tree in full bloom. You don't have a companion with you. Hey foolish girl, aren't you afraid of rogues?

231. [Nun:] Hey Māra, even if hundreds and thousands of rogues were to come here, not even a single hair on my body will shake or rise from fear. Hey Māra, why are you worried that I am alone?

232. Hey Māra, know this: I can disappear right in front of you or I can enter into your belly or I can stand between your eyebrows and you will not be able to see me standing there.

233. I have mastery over my mind. I have also well-developed the bases of psychic powers. I have achieved the six supernormal knowledges. The Buddha's path has been fully followed by me.

234. Sensual pleasures are like poisoned weapons. Aggregates of clinging are like pieces of rotten flesh. What you call "delight in sensual pleasures" is "non-delight" for me.

235. Desire for everything has been destroyed by me. The dark mass of ignorance has been torn apart.

Māra, know that you are defeated.

These verses were said by Arahant Nun Uppalavaṇṇā.

Section of Sixteen Verses

The verses of Arahant Nun Puṇṇā

236. [Maid Puṇṇā:] I am a maid who carries water. Fearing punishment and the insults of my house owner, I have always gone down to the river to get water, even in the coldest of weather. I didn't want to get blamed for any error.

237. But, Brāhmin, who do you fear that makes you go down to the river every morning and evening? It's so cold that your body shivers.

238. [Brāhmin:] Puṇṇā, why do you ask me this when you already know the answer? When I'm at the river, I am washing away evil and performing wholesome deeds.

239. Whoever young or old has committed any evil action is able to be freed from evil by bathing in water.

240. [Maid Puṇṇā:] Brāhmin, you have no idea about the results of kamma. Who is the ignorant person who taught that you can be freed from evil by bathing in water? He doesn't know and doesn't see the results of kamma.

241. Now listen. If your opinion is true, then all frogs, turtles, alligators, crocodiles and all water creatures will absolutely go to heaven.

242. If your opinion is true, then all sheep butchers, pig butchers, fishermen, animal abusers, thieves, executioners, and other evil doers are all able to be freed from their evil actions by bathing in water.

243. If these rivers wash away the evil you previously did, then won't it wash away your merit too? In that case you would be without merit too!

244. Brāhmin, every day you go down to the river fearing evil, don't you? In that case, just don't do bad things. Don't let the cold strike your skin!

245. [Brāhmin:] Oh wise girl! I had entered upon the wrong path, but you have guided me onto the noble path by rescuing me from this pointless bathing. I will give you this piece of cloth as a gift.

246-9. [Puṇṇā:] Keep the piece of cloth for yourself. I don't want it. If you are afraid of suffering, if suffering is unpleasant to you, do not commit evil actions either openly or in secret. But if you commit or will commit evil actions, then there is no escape from suffering, even if you try to run away and hide from the result. If you are afraid of suffering, if suffering is unpleasant for you, then go for refuge to the Buddha who has an unshaken mind, the Dhamma and the Saṅgha. Observe the precepts. These will definitely lead to your well-being.

250. [Brāhmin:] I will go for refuge to the Buddha who has an unshaken mind, the Dhamma and the Saṅgha. I will observe the precepts. These will definitely lead to my well-being.

251. Previously, I was called Brahmabandhu because I was born into the clan of Brāhmins. But now I am truly a Brāhmin. I attained the Triple Knowledge. I achieved Nibbāna. I entered wholesomeness and I am washed clean.

These verses were said by Arahant nun Puṇṇā.

Section of Twenty Verses

The verses of Arahant Nun Ambapāli

252. In the past my hair was black, like the color of bees, with curly ends. But because of old age, now it is like dried, rotten bark. The words of the truth speaker, the Buddha, aren't false.

253. In the past, my hair was fragrant, covered in flowers like a perfumed books. But because of old age, now it smells like a rabbit's fur. The words of the truth speaker, the Buddha, aren't false.

254. I used to comb my hair like a beautiful, neatly planted flowerbed. I used to untangle all knots and decorate my hair with golden pins. But because of old age, now my hair is thinning and falling out. The words of the truth speaker, the Buddha, aren't false.

255. Possessing golden pins, decorated with golden ornaments, adorned with plaits, it looked beautiful. But because of old age, my head is now bald. The words of the truth speaker, the Buddha, aren't false.

256. In the past, my eyebrows looked beautiful, like well painted crescents made by artists. But because of old age they now droop down with wrinkles. The words of the truth speaker, the Buddha, aren't false.

257. My eyes were large and black. They shined brilliantly like jewels. But overwhelmed by old age, they no longer look beautiful. The words of the truth speaker, the Buddha, aren't false.

258. In the bloom of my youth, my nose was delicate and peaked. It made my face look beautiful. But because of old age, now my nose is drooped down. The words of the truth speaker, the Buddha, aren't false.

259. In the past, my earlobes looked beautiful, like well fashioned and well finished bracelets. But because of old age, they now droop down with wrinkles. The words of the truth speaker, the Buddha, aren't false.

260. In the past, my teeth looked beautiful, like the color of the pure white bud of the banana tree. But because of old age, they now are broken and yellow. The words of the truth speaker, the Buddha, aren't false.

261. I used to have a sweet voice, like a sweet humming bird wandering among bushes and shrubs in the forest. But because of old age, it now stutters and lags. The words of the truth speaker, the Buddha, aren't false.

262. In the past, my neck looked beautiful, like a well rubbed, delicate golden shell. But because of old age, it is now hunched and wrinkled. The words of the truth speaker, the Buddha, aren't false.

263. In the past, both my arms looked beautiful, like they were made of gold. But because of old age, now they are weak and bony, just like the branches of the pātali tree. The words of the truth speaker, the Buddha, aren't false.

264. In the past, my fingers looked beautiful, decorated with delicate golden rings. But because of old age, now they look like the roots of onions and radishes. The words of the truth speaker, the Buddha, aren't false.

265. In the past, my breasts looked beautiful, lifted up, round and close together. But now they hang down like empty water bags. The words of the truth speaker, the Buddha, aren't false.

266. In the past, my body looked beautiful, like a well-polished sheet of gold. But now it is covered with drooping skin. The words of the truth speaker, the Buddha, aren't false.

267. In the past, both my thighs looked beautiful, like the shape of an elephant's graceful trunk. But because of old age, they are now like stalks of dried bamboo. The words of the truth speaker, the Buddha, aren't false.

268. In the past, my calves look beautiful, decorated with delicate golden anklets. But because of old age, they are now like the stalks of vegetables. The words of the truth speaker, the Buddha, aren't false.

269. In the past, the soles of my feet were soft and looked beautiful, like shoes full of cotton. But because of old age, they are now cracked and wrinkled. The words of the truth speaker, the Buddha, aren't false.

270. Such is the true nature of this body. The body loses its dignity with old age. It is the home of many pains. Now this body is like a broken down house, beyond repair, about to fall apart. The words of the truth speaker, the Buddha, aren't false.

These verses were said by Arahant Nun Ambapāli.

The verses of Arahant Nun Rohiṇī

271. [Father:] My dear daughter, you go to sleep praising monks. You wake up praising monks. You always praise the good qualities of monks. Do you also wish to be a nun?

272. You offer abundant food and drink to the monks. Rohiṇī, now I ask you; why do you like those monks so much?

273. These monks are inactive, they're lazy, and they live only on what is given by others. They expect things from others and always desire good things. Why do you like these monks so much?

274. [Rohiṇī:] My dear father, only now, after a long time, you have questioned me about the monks. I will now tell you about their wisdom, virtue and effort.

275. They are truly active and not lazy. They are the doers of the best actions. They work to abandon desire and hatred. That is why I like the monks.

276. They shake off the three roots of evil. They are doers of pure actions. All their evil has been eliminated. That is why I like the monks.

277. Their bodily actions are pure, as are their verbal actions. Their mental actions are also pure. That is why I like the monks.

278. Like pearls, they are spotless and purified internally and externally. They are full of wholesome qualities. That is why I like the monks.

279. They have heard many teachings of the Buddha. They have also memorized them well. They are noble and live in accordance with the Dhamma. They teach the Dhamma and are able to explain the meanings profoundly. That is why I like the monks.

280. They have heard many teachings of the Buddha. They have also memorized them well. They are noble and live in accordance with the Dhamma. They are mindful and possess one-pointedness of the mind. That is why I like the monks.

281. They travel in search of faraway monasteries. They are mindful, speak moderately and are not conceited. They understand the end of suffering, Nibbāna. That is why I like the monks.

282. If they leave a village, they do not look back longingly at anything. Indeed they go without longing. That is why I like the monks.

283. They do not store their property in storerooms, or in a pot, or in a basket. They only seek food cooked by families. That is why I like the monks.

284. They do not accept gold, silver or money. They live satisfied with whatever necessities are available at the time. That is why I like the monks.

285. Coming from various families and places, they have become monks. Nevertheless, they are friendly to one another. That is why I like the monks.

286. [Father:] My dear daughter, truly you were born to our family for our benefit. You have confidence in the Buddha and the Dhamma, and have keen reverence for the community of monks.

287. You have indeed recognized the unsurpassed field of merit. When these monks accept our gifts, that offering will bring great benefit to us.

288. [Rohiṇī:] Dear father, if you are afraid of suffering, and if suffering is unpleasant for you, you should go for refuge to the Buddha, the one with an unshakable mind; to the Dhamma; and to the community of monks. Observe the precepts which will lead to your well-being.

289. [Father:] Yes, my dear daughter, I will go for refuge to the Buddha, the one with an unshakable mind; to the Dhamma, and to the community of monks. I will observe the precepts which will lead to my well-being.

290. Previously, I was called Brahmabandhu—the relative of Brāhmins—because I was born into the clan of Brāhmins. But now I am truly a Brāhmin. I attained the Triple Knowledge. I achieved Nibbāna. I have mastered the Dhamma. I entered the goodness. I am washed clean.

These verses were said by Arahant Nun Rohiṇī

The verses of Arahant Nun Cāpā

291. [Upaka:] Formerly, I was an ascetic wandering around with a pot and stick. But now I am a deer hunter. Because of craving, I haven't been able to cross the swamp of sensual pleasures to reach the far shore.

292. Cāpā thinks that I am still attracted to her. She is cradling our son. But having cut the bond I had between Cāpā and myself, I will become a monk again.

293. [Cāpā:] My great hero, don't be angry with me. My great sage, don't be angry with me. For there is no purity for one overcome by anger, let alone the virtues of an ascetic.

294. [Upaka:] I shall indeed leave this village of Nālā. Who will live here in Nālā? It was this female figure that kept ascetics from living righteously.

295. [Cāpā:] Come Kāla Upaka, turn back! Enjoy sensual pleasures as you did before! My relatives and I are astounded by you.

296. [Upaka:] Cāpā, even if one quarter of your admiration is expressed to a man who is attached to you, your appreciation will seem huge to him.

297. [Cāpā:] Kāla, there is a blooming takkārī tree on the peak of a mountain. There is a blooming pomegranate tree. There is a blooming pāṭalī tree in the middle of an island.

298. My body is smeared with red sandal-wood cream. I am wearing the best clothes from Kāsi. As I am very beautiful, how can you leave me, ignoring this beauty?

299. [Upaka:] A bird hunter wants to trap and capture birds. You are trying to do the same, but you will not capture me by your beauty.

300. [Cāpā:] Kāla, look at our son I obtained from you. Leaving me with our son, how can you abandon us?

301. [Upaka:] Wise men leave their sons, relatives, and wealth. Breaking all fetters, those great heroes become monks, like an elephant that has broken its chains.

302. [Cāpā:] Ah, I see. Then, I will now murder our son with a stick or a knife on the spot, or I will knock him down to the ground. Because of grief for your son, you will not go.

303. [Upaka:] Hey wretched lady, even if you throw our son into a pit of hungry wolves and dogs, you will not turn me back again for the sake of our son.

304. [Cāpā:] Kāla, my darling husband, then tell me where you are going. To which village, town, city, or kingdom are you going?

305. [Upaka:] Formerly, we were leaders of ascetic groups. Not being true recluses, we only pretended to be so. We wandered from village to village, city to city, and from kingdom to kingdom.

306. But this time it is different. Alongside the river Nerañjara the Blessed One, the Buddha Gotama, teaches the Dhamma to beings for the eradication of all suffering. This time, I shall go to the Buddha's presence. The Buddha will be my Great Teacher.

307. [Cāpā:] Ah! Please tell the unsurpassed protector of the world that I worship him. Yes, worship respectfully and dedicate the merit to me.

308. [Upaka:] Yes, as you say Cāpā, you can receive that merit. I will tell the unsurpassed protector of the world that you worshipped him. Having worshiped him, I will surely dedicate the merit to you.

309. Then Kāḷa went out alongside the river Nerañjara. He saw the Supremely Enlightened Buddha teaching about the deathless state, Nibbāna.

310. That Dhamma is about suffering, the arising of suffering, the overcoming of suffering and the Noble Eightfold Path that leads to the cessation of suffering.

311. He worshipped the sacred feet of the Great Teacher. Having worshipped him respectfully, he dedicated the merit to Cāpā. He became a monk. He achieved the Triple Knowledge. The Buddha's path has been fully followed by him.

These verses were said by Arahant Nun Cāpā.

The verses of Arahant Nun Sundarī

312. [Brāhmin:] Lady, in your previous lives you survived by eating your dead children. You mourned excessively day and night.

313. Brāhmin lady Vāseṭṭhī, having eaten hundreds of your dead children, why don't you mourn them greatly today?

314. [Lady Vāseṭṭhī:] Brāhmin, it is not only me, in your previous lives, you too have eaten hundreds of your children and relatives.

315. But in this life, I have realized the escape from birth and death. Therefore, I do not grieve or lament, nor do I mourn.

316. [Brāhmin:] Vāseṭṭhī, you are saying something amazing. Whose Dhamma have you realized to speak firmly like this?

317. [Vāseṭṭhī:] Brāhmin, back then the Supremely Enlightened Buddha visited the city of Mithilā. He was teaching the Dhamma to beings for the eradication of all suffering.

318. Brāhmin, I heard the Dhamma from the Buddha about the end of defilements. Having realized the perfect Dhamma, I thrust away the grief for my children.

319. [Brāhmin:] Ah! I too shall go to the city of Mithilā. It would be good if the Blessed One would release me from all suffering.

320. The Brāhmin met the Buddha who was liberated and freed from defilements. The Great Sage, the Buddha, who reached the far shore of suffering taught him the Dhamma. That Dhamma is about suffering, the arising of suffering, the overcoming of suffering and the Noble Eightfold Path leading to the cessation of suffering.

321. He realized the perfect Dhamma. His only wish was to become a monk. Within three nights, the Brāhmin Sujāta attained the Triple Knowledge.

322. Come, dear charioteer. Now go home and return this chariot to the Brāhmin lady. Tell her I am in good health and that the

Brāhmin Sujāta has now become a monk and within three nights he attained the Triple Knowledge.

323. Then that charioteer took the chariot and a thousand gold coins and met the Brāhmin lady. He informed her that the Brāhmin was in good health, had become a monk, and within three nights attained the Triple Knowledge.

324. [Brāhmin lady:] Dear charioteer, since I heard from you that the Brāhmin has attained the Triple Knowledge, I give you this horse, chariot and a thousand gold coins as a gift of blessings.

325. [Charioteer:] Oh Brāhmin lady, keep the horse, chariot, and the thousand gold coins for yourself. I too will go and become a monk in the presence of the Buddha who has excellent wisdom.

326. [Brāhmin lady:] My dear daughter, Sundarī, your father has become a monk, abandoning his elephants, cows and horses, jewels and ornaments, lands and wealth. Now enjoy this wealth. You are the heir of our family.

327. [Sundarī:] My dear mother, abandoning elephants, cows and horses, jewels and ornaments, lands and wealth, my father has become a monk because he was troubled by the sorrow of his son's death. I too shall become a nun, as I am troubled by sorrow over my brother's death.

328. [Brāhmin lady:] My dear daughter, Sundarī, if you only wish to become a nun, may that noble intention come true! Once you become a nun you will survive on house-to-house alms food. You will wear a rag robe. Be content with these and become liberated from taints.

329. [Sundarī:] Venerable elder nun, I was still a trainee then. I purified my divine eye. I knew about my previous lives through the knowledge of recollecting past lives.

330. Venerable elder nun, you are my noble friend. Full of virtues, you beautify the community of nuns. It is because of your help

that I attained the Triple Knowledge. The Buddha's path has been fully followed by me.

331. Venerable elder nun, I wish to go to Sāvatthi; please allow me to go. I shall roar a lion's roar in the presence of the excellent Buddha.

332. [Elder nun:] Sundarī, then go and see the Great Teacher who shines with golden colored skin. You can see the tamer of the untamed beings, the Buddha, who has no fear at all.

333. Sundarī, go and see the Buddha who is liberated from all suffering and defilements. He is desireless and detached from craving. Eradicating taints, the Buddha has completed the path to end suffering.

334. [Sundarī to Buddha:] Great Hero, having left the city of Bārāṇasī I have come to see you. I am your disciple Sundarī. I worship your sacred feet.

335. Enlightened One, you are the Buddha, you are the Great Teacher, and I am your daughter. I was born from your heart, and born from your Dhamma path. Eradicating all taints, I have completed the path to end suffering.

336. [The Buddha:] Fortunate nun, it is good that you visited me. Your visit is not unbeneficial. Your behaviour matches the way of tamed disciples. Eradicating desire and taints, being detached from craving, and having completed the path, such disciples visit the Great Teacher and worship his sacred feet.

These verses were said by Arahant Nun Sundarī.

The verses of Arahant Nun Subhā, the smith's daughter

337. Back then, when I was very young, wearing a white dress, I went to listen to the Dhamma. While listening to the Dhamma vigilantly, I obtained the realization of the Noble Truths that day.

338. From then on, I developed non-delight in all sensual pleasures. I was afraid of craving for repeated existence. My only wish was to become a nun.

339. I left my relatives, slaves, and servants, fertile fields and lands. I left all delightful and pleasant possessions.

340. In this way, I abandoned great wealth and became a nun. This Dhamma path is truly well proclaimed. I became a nun with much faith in the Buddha. Therefore, it would not be fitting for me to desire gold and silver again. My only desire is ultimate freedom, Nibbāna.

341. If one takes gold and silver after laying them aside, it would be a huge mistake! Gold and silver are not conducive to enlightenment or peace. Furthermore it is not proper for recluses. Gold and silver are not the noble wealth.

342. Sensual pleasures only generate greed and intoxication. They cause delusion and only increase defilements. They cause one's life to be filled with suspicions and many troubles. Truly, there is no permanent stability in sensual pleasures.

343. People become infatuated with sensual pleasures, engage in evil actions, and defile their minds. Then they envy each other and start quarrels.

344. Those people who have fallen into sensual pleasures are engaged in slaughtering and harming. They are struck by sadness, sorrow, grief, despair and misery.

345. Oh, dear relatives, why, like enemies, do you urge me towards sensual pleasures? Please understand that I became a nun because I saw fear in sensual pleasures.

346. Taints are not eradicated by means of gold and money. Sensual pleasures are enemies, murderers, and hostile beings. They bind minds to the arrow of sorrow.

347. Oh, dear relatives, why, like my enemies, do you urge me towards sensual pleasures? Please understand that with a shaven head and rag robes I have become a nun.

348. I survive on house-to-house alms food and wear rag robes. These requisites are indeed proper for me since I have renounced the world.

349. Great Seers reject all sensual pleasures, whether human or divine. They are well-established in the place of security. With liberated minds, they have arrived at an unshakable happiness.

350. I don't want to have any relationship with sensual pleasures, in which no protection is found. Sensual pleasures are like enemies, murderers, and volcanoes. They are painful.

351. Sensual pleasures are a terror, and affliction. They are thorns. They are disgusting and disagreeable. They are a great cause of delusion.

352. Sensual pleasures are like a frightful attack, like a snake's head. The ignorant, ordinary, foolish people delight in them.

353. The people who are attached to the mud of sensual pleasures are ignorant. They never understand the end of the cycle of birth and death.

354. Because of sensual pleasures, people have entered the ways that lead to the planes of misery. They have entered the way that bring them diseases.

355. In this way, sensual pleasures are enemy-producing, burning, and defiling. They lure and ensnare one towards defilements and death.

356. Sensual pleasures make people jabber. They are maddening, agitating the mind and defiling beings. They are traps set by Māra.

357. Sensual pleasures have endless miseries, they have immense pain, they are strong poisons, they give little enjoyment, they arouse lust, and they dry up the wholesome part of life.

358. Since I have understood the tragedy caused by sensual pleasures, I shall not return to them again; I shall always delight in ultimate freedom, Nibbāna.

359. I wish for the cool state, liberation. I have abandoned sensual desire. Having destroyed all fetters, I live diligently.

360. The Great Seers crossed over the journey of rebirths by following the Noble Eightfold Path. I also follow that sorrowless, stainless, secure, straight way.

361. Look at this Subhā, the smith's daughter, establishing her mind in the Dhamma. She has attained the end of craving. She meditates at the foot of a tree.

362. Today is the eighth day since Subhā became a nun. She was instructed by the faithful nun Uppalavaṇṇā who became beautiful by means of Dhamma, and attained the Triple Knowledge leaving Māra behind.

363. This nun Subhā is flawless, without debt, with developed faculties, released from all ties. She has completed the path and is without taints.

364. Sakka, the leader of gods, approaching by psychic powers with a group of deities, worships that Subhā, the smith's daughter.

These verses were said by Arahant Nun Subhā, the smith's daughter.

Section of Thirty Verses

The verses of Arahant Nun Subhā, who dwelled in the Jīvaka mango garden

365. On one occasion, the nun Subhā was going to the delightful Jīvaka mango garden. Then suddenly a rogue appeared and stood blocking her way. Subhā said this to him:

366. What wrong have I done to you, that you should stand there blocking my way? It is not fitting, sir, that a man should touch a nun.

367. I deeply respect the Buddha's path. The Sublime One has taught us about the precepts. I protect those precepts purely. I am taintless. So, why are you standing here blocking me?

368. You have a disturbed mind. My mind is undisturbed. You are a defiled person. I am a taintless person with no lust. I am liberated from every single defilement. So, why are you standing here blocking me?

369. [Rogue:] You are still young. You are not ugly. What good will nunhood do for you? Throw away your robe. Come, let's enjoy ourselves in this forest full of blooms.

370. The blooming shrubs release a sweet smell in all directions with the pollen of their flowers. This is the beginning of spring and the weather is very comfortable. Come, let us enjoy ourselves in this forest full of blooms.

371. The trees with blossoming crests sway in the wind as if they were singing and dancing. You have entered this forest alone. What enjoyment is here for you?

372. This fearful forest is inhabited by herds of animals and sur-rounded by female and male elephants. In this frightening great forest, do you wish to walk alone without a companion?

373. Your beauty is beyond compare. You are like a statue of gold decorated by the finest Kāsi cloth. Oh, incomparable one, you shine with beauty like a decorated golden statue. You are like an angel in the Cittalata forest.

374. I am dazzled by your beauty. If we both were to live together in this forest, I would devote my life to you. Oh, you have crystal clear, shining eyes like that of an angel. There is no other person dearer to me than you.

375. If you will grant my bidding, come and live happily with me in my house. I will offer you my luxurious palace, and servant girls, who will always attend to your needs.

376. Then you will wear Kāsi, the finest of all clothes, and put on flower garlands and perfumes. I will make you many ornaments of gold, jewels, and pearls.

377. In that palace there is a bed made of sandalwood with a comfortable mattress and a well-washed, beautiful coverlet. It is spread with a new, costly woolen quilt. You can sleep very peace-fully on this fragrant bed.

378. So, why are you living this life of a nun? It is like a blue lotus lake possessed by a demon. Because of your celibate life, you will grow old with your limbs untouched by any man.

379. [Subhā:] What is it that you consider substantial here in this body, which is full of filth, filling the cemetery, and is destined to break up? What is it that you appreciate so much when you look at this body?

380. [Rogue:] It is your eyes that I appreciate. Your eyes are extremely beautiful, like those of a doe, like those of a nymph

who lives between mountains. When I see your eyes my desire for sensual pleasures increases all the more.

381. You are like a golden statue. The eyes on your face can be compared with the petals of a red lotus. By seeing your eyes, my desire for sensual pleasures increases all the more.

382. You, the one with big eyes, you, the one with the pure gaze, no eyes are dearer to me than yours, you nymph with pleasant eyes. Even if you go far away, I shall always remember your eyes.

383. [Subhā:] No, you wish to go by the wrong path! You seek to have the moon as a toy. You wish to jump over mount Meru. Understand me, the one you wish for is a daughter of the Buddha.

384. In this world with its gods, nothing can arouse lust in me. I don't know what lust is anymore. By following the path of Nibbāna, I have rooted out lust.

385. Like sparks from a pit of burning coals cooling down, like destroying a bowl of poison, I destroyed lust. By following the path of Nibbāna, I have rooted out lust.

386. You may seduce a woman who is not insightful or who hasn't seen the Buddha through the Dhamma, but not me. You bother me, as I have realized the true nature of life.

387. Whether I am insulted or praised, in both happiness and unhappiness, my mindfulness is well established. I have understood that all conditioned things are disgusting. My mind does not cling to anything at all.

388. I'm a disciple of the Buddha. I travel in the vehicle called the Noble Eight Fold Path. I have pulled out the dart of lust and destroyed the taints. My heart only delights in an empty hut.

389. I have seen well painted wooden puppets, fastened by strings and sticks. They dance in various ways.

390. If these strings and sticks are removed, thrown away, scattered, and broken into pieces, then there is no puppet in them whatsoever. In which part of them should one delight?

391. This body is also like a puppet. It does not exist without supporting factors. As it does not exist without supporting factors, in which part of the body should one delight?

392. Just as you see a picture painted on a wall of a woman colored with paints, if people mistake it for a real woman, it is because their perception is distorted.

393. You are blind. You run after an empty thing which is like an illusion placed before you by a magician. You are after a golden tree someone had in a dream. You are like playing in a puppet show in the midst of the people.

394. These eyes are like little balls set in hollow grooves, with a bubble in the middle, smeared with tears. Inside these grooves there are eye secretions, various sorts of tendons, and flesh rolled into balls.

395. The good looking lady, Subhā, was not attached to her eyes. With an unattached mind, Subhā suddenly tore out one of her eyes. She said, "Come, take this eye for yourself," and straight away she gave it to the man.

396-97. Instantly, the rogue's lust ceased and he begged her pardon. [Rogue:] "Oh celibate nun, may you recover soon! Such a thing will not happen again. If one tries to attack a noble nun like this, it is like embracing a blazing fire. It is like grabbing a poisonous snake with your bare hands. That person won't gain any happiness. Please forgive me."

398. The nun was freed from the rogue and went to the excellent Buddha. The very instant she saw the one with great marks of

excellent merit, the Buddha, her eye was restored to its former condition.

These verses were said by Arahant Nun Subhā, who dwelled in the Jīvaka mango garden.

Section of Forty Verses

The verses of Arahant Nun Isidāsī

399. The city of Pāṭaliputta, which is known as the Kusuma kingdom, is like an ornament for the entire earth. Two nuns who were born into the Sākyan clan possessed good qualities and they were living in that city.

400. One of those nuns was named Isidāsī; the second one was named Bodhī. Both were very virtuous. Both delighted in meditation and had memorized the Buddha's teaching well. They had shaken off their defilements.

401. One day, they went on their alms round and had their meal. After washing their bowls, they sat happily in a secluded place. On that occasion, this conversation took place:

402. [Bodhī:] Noble Isidāsī, you are gorgeous and you are still in the prime of your youth. What fault did you see in the household life that made you become a nun?

403. Asked in this way in a secluded place, Isidāsī, who was skilful in the teaching of the Dhamma, replied: "Then, Bodhī, listen to how I became a nun."

404. [Isidāsī:] My father was a wealthy merchant in the city Ujjenī. He was restrained by virtue. I was his only daughter, dear, charming and beloved.

405. Once, from the city of Sāketa, a marriage was proposed to me from a high-caste family. That man was also a wealthy merchant. My father gave me away to that family as their new daughter in-law.

406. From then on, every morning and evening, approaching my mother-in-low and father-in-law, I worshiped their feet. I obeyed every rule they commanded.

407. Every time I saw my husband's sisters, brothers, and his other family members, I would immediately stand up and give them my seat.

408. I satisfied them with food, drink, sweets, and anything they desired. I served them as best as I could.

409. I attended to their every need. When my husband arrived, I would wash his feet. When I approached him, I always worshiped him with joined palms.

410. Taking a comb, perfumes, jewelry and a mirror, I myself adorned my husband as though I was a servant-girl.

411. I prepared the rice myself. I washed the dishes myself. I looked after my husband as a mother looks after her only son.

412. Though I lived attending to every need of my husband and worked hard like a servant, organizing everything humbly, not being lazy, and being virtuous, my husband would scold me angrily.

413. He said to his mother and father, "I will leave this house and go. I won't have anything to do with this family life together with Isidāsī."

414. [Parents:] Do not speak in this way son. Isidāsī is undoubtedly a smart and lucky wife. She has always been energetic and never lazy. This being the case, why are you so displeased with Isidāsī?

415. [Husband:] Yes, she has done no harm to me but I will not live with Isidasī. She is extremely boring. I have had enough of her. I will leave this house without telling any of you.

416. Hearing his words, my father-in-law and mother-in-law asked me, "What offense have you committed? Tell us truthfully what you have done."

417. [Isidāsī:] I haven't offended him at all. I have not harmed him, or said any harsh words to him. What can I do when my husband hates me?

418. Overcome by grief and pain, his parents led me back to my father's house, saying, "We have lost the goddess of fortune, who kept our son safe."

419. This time, my father gave me in marriage to a wealthy family who earned half of what my father did.

420. Just like before, I only lived in their house for a month, then he too rejected me, although I served him like a slave-girl, not harming him, and possessed of virtue.

421. Finally my father brought home a man who lived by begging food from others, and told him, "Throw away your rags and plate. Be my son-in-law."

422. He also lived with me for only a short time, and then said to my father, "Give back my rags, pot, and cup. I am going to live by begging again."

423. Then my father, mother, and all of my relatives told him: "What have we not done for you here in this house? Tell us what you want and we can arrange that for you in a minute."

424. Spoken to in this way, he said: "I am very well strong enough to live on my own. I have had enough with Isidāsī. I don't want to live together with her under the same roof."

425. I allowed him to go and he departed. All alone, I thought to myself, "Without taking leave from anyone I must go and commit suicide or become a nun."

426. In my city, there lived a noble nun named Jinadattā, who was an expert in the discipline, was well learned in the Dhamma,

and possessed virtue. She came to my father's house on her alms round.

427. Seeing her in our house, I rose up from my seat and offered it to her. She sat down and I worshipped her feet and I offered her food.

428. I served her with food, drink, sweets and whatever was prepared at my house. Then I said to her: "Noble nun, I too wish to become a nun."

429. Then my father said to me: "My dear daughter, practice the Dhamma while living at home. Serve recluses with food and drinks."

430. I fell down crying at my father's feet. Worshipping, I said to him: "No, I am experiencing the result of my own bad actions done by me alone. Let me destroy this evil."

431. Then my father said to me, "The best of humans, the Buddha, attained the greatest goal, Nibbāna. May you also attain the greatest goal, enlightenment, Nibbāna."

432. I worshiped my father, mother, and the community of my relatives. I became a nun. Seven days after becoming a nun, I attained the Triple Knowledge.

433. I can recollect my last seven births; the pain I have been experiencing was a result of an evil action done by me in those past lives. I will explain it to you, please listen attentively.

434. Seven lives ago, in the city of Erakaccha, I was a wealthy gold-smith. Intoxicated by pride in my youth, I engaged in sexual misconduct with the wives of others.

435. When I passed away from that life, I immediately fell into hell. I was boiled in hell for a long time. Once I escaped from the life in hell, I was reborn in the womb of a female monkey.

436. Seven days after my birth an elder monkey, the leader of the herd, castrated me. This was the result of that evil action of seducing the wives of others.

437. I passed away from that life and I was reborn in the womb of a one-eyed, lame female goat in the Sindhava forest.

438. There too I was castrated. I walked for twelve years carrying kids on my back. My wound was worm infested and the disease worsened. This was the result of that evil action of seducing the wives of others.

439. I passed away from that life and was reborn in the womb of a cow belonging to a cattle dealer. I was a reddish calf. In the twelfth month after my birth, I was castrated.

440. I ploughed the earth dragging a heavy plow and pulling a heavy cart. I became blind and diseased. This was the result of that evil action of seducing the wives of others.

441. I passed away from that life and I was reborn as a homeless street child. I was neither a woman nor a man. This was the result of that evil action of seducing the wives of others.

442. I died in my thirtieth year. I suffered a lot. I was reborn as a little girl into a poor carter's family that had little wealth and was greatly oppressed by creditors.

443. Then, because of their large unpaid debt, a caravan leader took me forcefully from my family and dragged me away screaming.

444. Then in my sixteenth year, the marriageable age, the caravan leader's son name Giridāsa took me as his wife.

445. He had another wife who was virtuous and possessed of good qualities. She was very loyal towards her husband. I became jealous of her and made our husband angry towards her.

446. It was my own sexual misconduct and jealousy that resulted in my husbands rejecting me, although I served them like a ser-

vant-girl. But now I have destroyed entirely all the results of all those evil actions.

These verses were said by Arahant Nun Isidāsī.

The Great Section

The verses of Arahant Nun Sumedhā

447. In the city of Mantāvatī, the daughter of King Koñca's chief queen was named Sumedhā. She was confident in the Buddha's path.

448. She was virtuous and her speech was sweet. She had memorized much Dhamma and was disciplined in the Buddha's path. One day, she went up to her mother and father and said: "Both of you, please listen to me."

449. I only delight in ultimate freedom. Even heavenly rebirth is not eternal, not to speak of human sensual pleasures. They are base, give little enjoyment, and come with much suffering.

450. Foolish people are intoxicated with sensual pleasures. But they are bitter, like a snake's poison. Chasing after sensual pleasures, those foolish people fall into hell and suffer for a long, long time.

451. Gaining knowledge that leads to harm, foolish people commit evil by body, speech, and mind. Then they fall into hell and sorrow greatly.

452. Those foolish people are unwise and are unable to think properly. They are enveloped in the arising of suffering and even if they are taught the Noble Truths they do not understand and realize them.

453. My dear mother, the majority of people in this world don't know the Four Noble Truths taught by the excellent Buddha. They long only for rebirth in heaven.

454. Everything included in existence is impermanent. Even rebirth among gods is non-eternal. But foolish people are not afraid of being reborn again and again.

455. For the most part, beings are reborn in the four planes of misery. Rebirth in the human and heavenly worlds is gained with much difficulty, but there is no living of the nun's life at all for those who have been born in planes of misery.

456. Therefore I ask that both of you give me your permission to become a nun in the path of the Buddha who possesses the ten powers. I will strive very hard for the elimination of birth and death.

457. What good will come to me by delighting in this existence? This body is indeed unsubstantial. I shall become a nun to achieve the cessation of the craving for existence. Please give me your permission.

458. A Buddha has appeared into the world in this era that we live in. I have avoided the occasions where I would have lost the opportunity of realizing the Dhamma. The moment when one should realize the Dhamma has been obtained by me. I will protect my virtuous and celibate life as long as I live.

459. Sumedhā spoke further to her mother and father and said, "If you don't permit me to become a nun, I will starve myself to death."

460. Feeling much pain, her mother started to cry. Her father, also full of tears, sought to dissuade Sumedhā as she lay on the mansion floor. Her father tried to arouse a desire in her to live the household life again.

461. [King:] "My dear daughter, please stand up! What benefit will you gain by being sad? Besides, you have been given in marriage to King Anīkadatta in the city of Vāraṇavatī. And most importantly, he is very handsome. You have been betrothed to him.

462. Once you become the wife of King Anīkadatta, you will be the chief queen. But, oh Daughter, protecting precepts, living a celibate life, and being a nun are difficult things to do.

463. With royal power you will be able to give orders. You will have authority over the family and wealth. All the enjoyments in the palace will be yours. Daughter, you are still young, enjoy sensual pleasures and let your marriage take place!"

464-65. Sumedhā spoke to them and said: "I don't need anything that's part of this unsubstantial existence! Either I will become a nun or die! There will be no marriage!"

465. This impure body is filthy, foul smelling, frightful, a heap of disgusting things, always oozing, and is like a bag filled with excrement. How can I enjoy such a filthy body?

466. This body, smeared with flesh and blood, is repulsive. I have realized the true nature of this body. It is a resort for worms, and food for vultures and other birds. To whom should I give such a body in marriage?

468. In the cemetery, this body will become food for dogs and wolves. After having thrown away this body in the cemetery, the mother and father of that person, disgusted with the dead body, bathe themselves. This is the unfortunate destiny of everybody.

469. The body is bound together with bones and tendons. It is filled with saliva, tears, excrement, and urine, but foolish people are attached to the body.

470. If anyone, dissecting it, were to turn this body inside out, even one's own mother, being unable to bear the foul smell of it, would be disgusted.

471. I am reflecting on the true nature of the five groups of clinging, the four elements, the six sense bases, things dependently arisen, and the suffering arisen from birth. While reflecting in this way, how can I wish for marriage?

472. The Buddha taught the simile that a person strikes another person with three hundred spears a day and in the end he guarantees the Dhamma realization to that person. Let me be struck by three hundred iron spears every day. Even if the striking lasts a hundred years, it would better for me if this was the way to the end of suffering.

473. In this way, even when one knows the words of the Great Teacher, if one delights in this tragedy of aging and death, one has to be born again and again. In this way their journey of misery gets prolonged.

474. Immeasurable suffering is seen in heaven, the human world, the animal world, the titan world, the ghost world, and hell.

475. If one falls into hell, the animal world, the titan world, and the ghost world, one has to suffer immensely. One doesn't have protection even among the gods; therefore there is nothing superior to the happiness of Nibbāna.

476. But those who follow the instruction of the ten-powered Buddha and strive for the elimination of birth and death can attain ultimate freedom, Nibbāna.

477. Dear father, this very day I will renounce the household life; what have I to do with this unsubstantial wealth? I gave up these sensual pleasures as if vomiting something up. I made my desire extinct, like a palm tree that has been cut down.

478. In this way she spoke to her father. In the meantime, King Anīkadatta, to whom she was promised, left the city of Vāranavati for the wedding.

479. Inside her room, Sumedhā cut off her soft, rich, black hair with a sword. With the door closed, she started meditating and reached the first meditative absorption.

480. She entered the jhāna well. King Anīkadatta arrived at the city of Mantāvatī. Sitting in the mansion, Sumedhā was skillfully developing the perception of impermanence.

481. While she was developing the perception of impermanence, King Anīkadatta, adorned with jewels and gold, quickly entered the mansion. Placing his hands together worshipping, he begged Sumedhā:

482. The authority, wealth, and all the enjoyments of the kingdom belong to you. You are still young. Enjoy sensual pleasures. In this world, happiness from sensual pleasures is hard to obtain.

483. Even rulership has been offered to you. Enjoy sensual pleasures and offer alms. Don't be depressed. Your mother and father are in great pain.

484. Sumedhā replied to him saying, "I have nothing to do with sensual pleasures. I am not deluded with them anymore. I tell you this: do not delight in sensual pleasures. See the danger in sensual pleasures.

485. Once in the past, there was a wheel-turning monarch named Mandhātu. He ruled over the four great continents. He was the foremost of those who enjoyed sensual pleasures. Even he died unsatisfied with his wishes unfulfilled.

486. Even if the seven-jewels-great-rain falls all around in the ten directions, still, there won't be satisfaction with sensual pleasures; indeed people die unsatisfied.

487. Sensual pleasures are like a butcher's knife and a heap of meat. Sensual pleasures are like a snake's head, they are like volcanoes, and they are like a bony skeleton.

488. Sensual pleasures are impermanent and unstable. They cause much suffering and are extremely painful. They are like a heated iron ball. Sensual pleasures are the root of all suffering. They have pain as the fruit.

489. Sensual pleasures are like the fruits of a tree being cut down. They are like lumps of flesh. They are painful. They are as if you were tricked in a dream. Sensual pleasures are like borrowed goods.

490. Sensual pleasures are like swords and sticks smeared with poison, like diseases, and are painful like a tumor. They take beings to death. They are dangerous like a charcoal pit. They are like an executioner.

491. In this way, sensual pleasures are said to cause much suffering, and are very dangerous. Therefore you may return home. I don't believe that anything belonging to self is found in this repeated existence.

492. What can someone do for me when his own head is burning? When one is followed closely by old age and death, one must strive to end them.

493. I opened the door. I saw my mother, father, and King Anīkadatta seated on the ground crying. I said to them:

494. The beginning of this journey of misery cannot be discovered. When foolish people repeatedly cry at the time of their father's death, at the tragedies of their brother, and at their own tragedies, this journey becomes prolonged for them.

495. In the long journey of repeated rebirth, recollect how many tears one has shed, the amount of mother's milk one has drunk, and the amount of blood one has shed. Recollect the size of the heap of bones of those beings who are journeying on.

496. The Buddha asked us to compare the tears we have shed to the water of the great oceans and the same with the amount of milk we have drunk. The Buddha asked us to recollect the heap of bones of a person as equal to the size of the mountain Vepulla.

497. Again the Buddha asked us to recollect the simile of splitting up the great earth into little clay balls the size of berries and

separating them, saying: "This ball represents my mother in this life, that ball represent my mother's mother." By this task, all the clay balls will be used up, but not the generations of mothers in this long journey of rebirth.

498. Also, the Buddha asked us to recollect the simile of splitting up all the trees, shrubs, and grass in this world into four-inch pieces and separate them, saying: "This piece represents my father in this life, that piece represents my father's father." By this task, all the pieces will be used up, but not the generations of fathers in this long journey of rebirth.

499. The Buddha asked us to recollect the simile of the blind turtle at the bottom of the great ocean who comes to the surface once every hundred years, puts its head through a small piece of wood with a hole in it and looks at the sky. Obtaining a human life is even more difficult.

500. The Buddha asked us to understand unsubstantial form as a lump of foam to understand the five groups of clinging as impermanent, and to recollect the immense suffering in hell.

501. He asked us to recollect how beings fill up the cemetery again and again as a result of being born in this life and that life. He asked us to recollect the greediness for food by comparing it to the simile of a person's fear when going into the water with a crocodile. He asked us to reflect on the Four Noble Truths.

502. At a time when the Buddha's Dhamma is available in the world, what is the point of chasing sensual pleasures? All the delights in sensual pleasures are extremely bitter.

503. At a time when the Buddha's Dhamma is available in the world and it is obvious that sensual pleasures are like a burning fever, what is the point of chasing sensual pleasures? All delights in sensual pleasures are like fire, unsubstantial, agitating, and burning.

504. This nun-life and monk-life don't bring enemies, but sensual pleasures bring many enemies. What use are sensual pleasures to you? Sensual pleasures are subject to destruction by kings, fire, thieves, floods, and undesirable people.

505. At a time when there is access to liberation, what is the use of sensual pleasures? Why do you create suffering, tragedies, and depression for yourself?

506. The grass torch burns the hand that grabs it, not the hand of the one who dropped it. Sensual pleasures are compared to a burning grass torch. As long as it is grabbed, it burns the holder.

507. Do not lose noble happiness for the sake of a little happiness from sensual pleasures! Do not suffer afterwards like a fish that has swallowed the hook!

508. Restrain your sense faculties from sensual pleasures. These beings have been bound by sensual pleasures like a dog that has been leashed by a chain. Like starving people slaughtering a dog, these sensual pleasures will do the same to you.

509. You are experiencing immeasurable pain and various distress of the mind due to your intoxication with sensual pleasures. Therefore, give up and abandon these sensual pleasures.

510. Wherever sensual pleasures exist, every birth and every existence is bound by old age, death, and sickness. At a time when unageing Nibbāna is available, what is the use of sensual pleasures?

511. Nibbāna is unageing and deathless. Nibbāna is the only base for the state of unageing and deathlessness. Nibbāna is the state that is devoid of sorrow, lamentation, obstructions, stains, fears, and depression.

512. Many attained deathless Nibbāna. Even today, if one reflects on the Dhamma as taught by the Buddha, one can attain Nibbāna. If one doesn't strive one won't attain it.

513. Sumedhā, not delighting in the conditioned world, spoke in this way. Getting the attention of King Anīkadatta, she threw her cut hair on the floor.

514. King Anīkadatta stood up with joined hands worshiping Sumedhā's father and begged him, "Let Sumedhā become a nun. May she attain the unshakeable liberation, the Noble Truth."

515. Her mother and father let her go. Frightened by sorrow and fear, Sumedhā became a nun. She attained the six supernormal knowledges while she was practicing the path as a trainee-nun. She attained the highest goal, liberation.

516. She started life as a princess, but now as a nun, her new experience of Nibbāna was an amazing and marvelous thing for her. In her last stage of life, through her ability to recollect past lives, she revealed the meritorious deeds that she had done in her previous lives.

517. "In the time of the Blessed One, Konāgamana, I built a monastery with my friends Dhananjāni and Khemā. We offered the monastery with its park and residence to the community of monks headed by the Buddha.

518. As a result of that merit, for ten times, one hundred times, a thousand times, and ten thousand times we were born among gods. What need is there to talk about rebirth among humans?

519. When we were among gods, we were very mighty and powerful. What need is there to talk about power when we were among humans? Once, I became the woman-jewel as the chief queen of the wheel-turning monarch who possessed seven jewels.

520. I gained all these wonders as a result of offering a monastery in the time of Konāgamana Buddha. That meritorious deed was the origin and that was the root. In this life, I experienced Nibbāna. Sumedhā, who delighted in the Dhamma, attained ultimate freedom.

521. Whoever places confirmed confidence in the words of the Buddha, who has incredible wisdom, and practices accordingly, will become disenchanted with everything included in existence. Having become disenchanted, they become liberated from everything."

These verses were said by Arahant Nun Sumedhā.

Index

Numbers refer to verse numbers for each Arahant.

Mahamegha English Publications

Sutta Translations
Stories of Sakka, Lord of Gods: Sakka Saṁyutta
Stories of Brahmas: Brahma Saṁyutta
Stories of Heavenly Mansions: Vimānavatthu
Stories of Ghosts: Petavatthu
The Voice Of Enlightened Monks: The Theragāthā
The Voice Of Enlightened Nuns: The Therīgāthā

Dhamma Books
The Wise Shall Realize

Children's Picture Books
The Life of the Buddha for Children
Chaththa Manawaka
Sumina the Novice Monk
Stingy Kosiya of Town Sakkara
Kisagothami
Kali the She-Devil
Ayuwaddana Kumaraya
Sumana the Florist
Sirigutta and Garahadinna
The Banker Anāthapiṇḍika
The Great Diciple Visakha

For more information visit www.mahamevnawa.ca

Mahamegha Publishers - Polgahawela

Tel : 037 2053300, 0773 216685 **e-mail** : mahameghapublishers@gmail.com

Thripitaka Sadaham Poth Madura - Borella

Tel : 0114 255 987, 077 4747161 **e-mail** : thripitakasadahambooks@gmail.com

Made in the USA
Middletown, DE
07 April 2017